INSTANT ART
for
BIBLE THEMES
WORKSHEETS

Book Two

Compiled by
Susan Sayers

Illustrated by
Helen Herbert

Kevin
Mayhew

First published in 1990 in Great Britain by
KEVIN MAYHEW LTD
Rattlesden
Bury St Edmunds, Suffolk IP30 0SZ

Catalogue No 1396027
ISBN 0 86209 530 1

© 1990 and 1994 Kevin Mayhew Ltd

Material in this book is copyright-free provided that it is used for the
purpose for which the book is intended. The usual copyright
restrictions apply to any use for *commercial* purposes.

Cover design by Roy Mitchell
Printed in Great Britain

Contents

Index of Uses

THE CHURCH: THE PEOPLE OF GOD

WORSHIP

THE CHURCH'S YEAR

BIBLICAL CHARACTERS

GOD TOLD MOSES "I WILL RESCUE MY PEOPLE!"

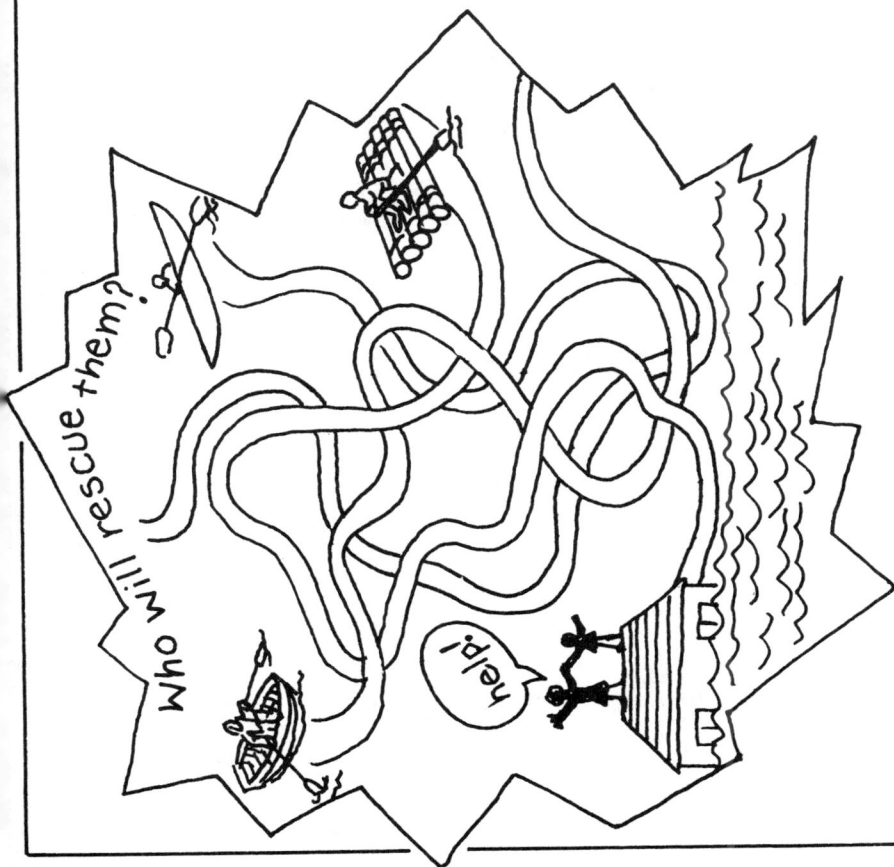

Find these words from the story:

MOSES
RESCUE
SLAVES
EGYPT
PROMISE
FREE
LEAD
PEOPLE

S	E	G	B	O	A	L	R
A	M	S	T	P	Y	G	E
P	S	O	I	C	G	P	S
E	L	J	S	M	B	L	C
O	A	C	H	E	O	F	U
P	V	N	K	E	S	R	E
L	E	A	D	R	D	C	P
E	S	E	R	F	I	M	Q

Exodus 6:2-8

Who will rescue them?

help!

We can always:

STROUSTINGSOLDO
ATBOOKHAEGLIPPING
BUSY

colour the dotted letters

JESUS IS BORN

Luke 2:8-20

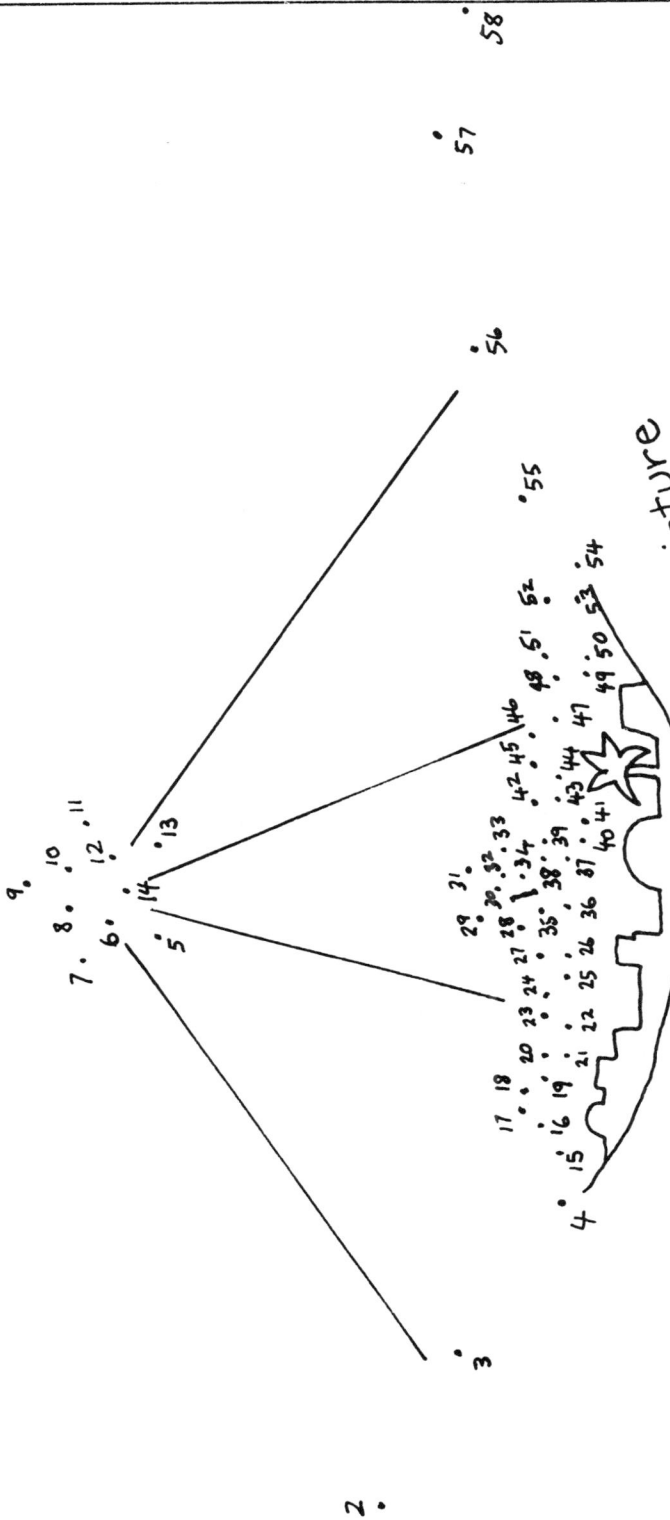

Join the dots, then colour the picture

Who were the first people to be told the good news?

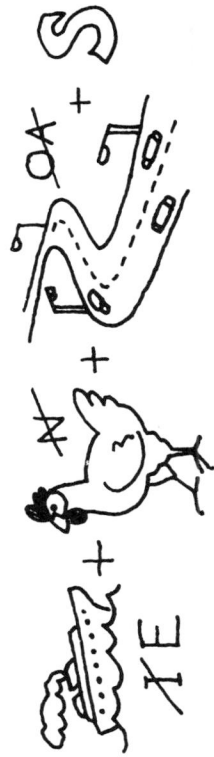

'GLORY TO GOD

IN THE HIGHEST'

SANG THE ANGELS

G	L	O	R	Y	A	B
M	U	N	S	A	N	G
D	O	G	E	D	G	C
O	B	H	N	F	E	E
T	T	J	I	A	L	H
H	I	G	H	E	S	T

THE WORK OF THE LORD IS FULL OF HIS GLORY

Ecclesiasticus 42:16

What does God's world tell us about God? He must be:

careful

wise

mean

powerful

loving

giving

selfish

dull

imaginative

Circle the right words

THE LORD HAS RESCUED US FROM DEATH!

1 Colossians 2:13-15

God to the rescue!
Who is he rescuing here?

FREEDOM.
FOR OUR
HIS DEATH PAID
~ SLAVES TO SIN
US FROM BEING
GOD RESCUES

GOD TO THE RESCUE!
WHO IS HE RESCUING HERE?

DRAW
A PICTURE
OF YOURSELF HERE

Exodus 6:2-13

GOD ELDERS HIS PEOPLE FROM
SLAVERY IN EGYPT HE IS RESCUING
(looking...)

Colour the picture

'TODAY', SAID JESUS,
'THIS WORD OF SCRIPTURE HAS
COME TRUE.'

Luke 4:14-21
and Isaiah 64:1-7

follow the strings to fit the words in

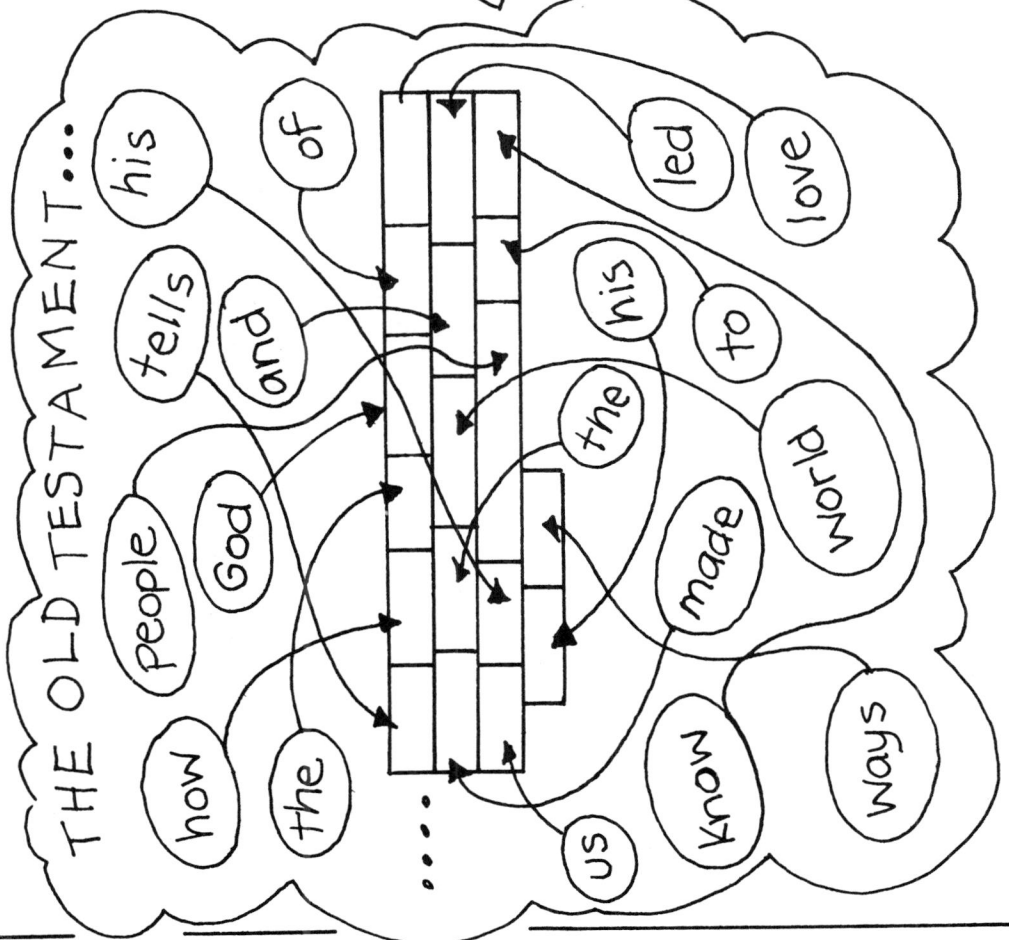

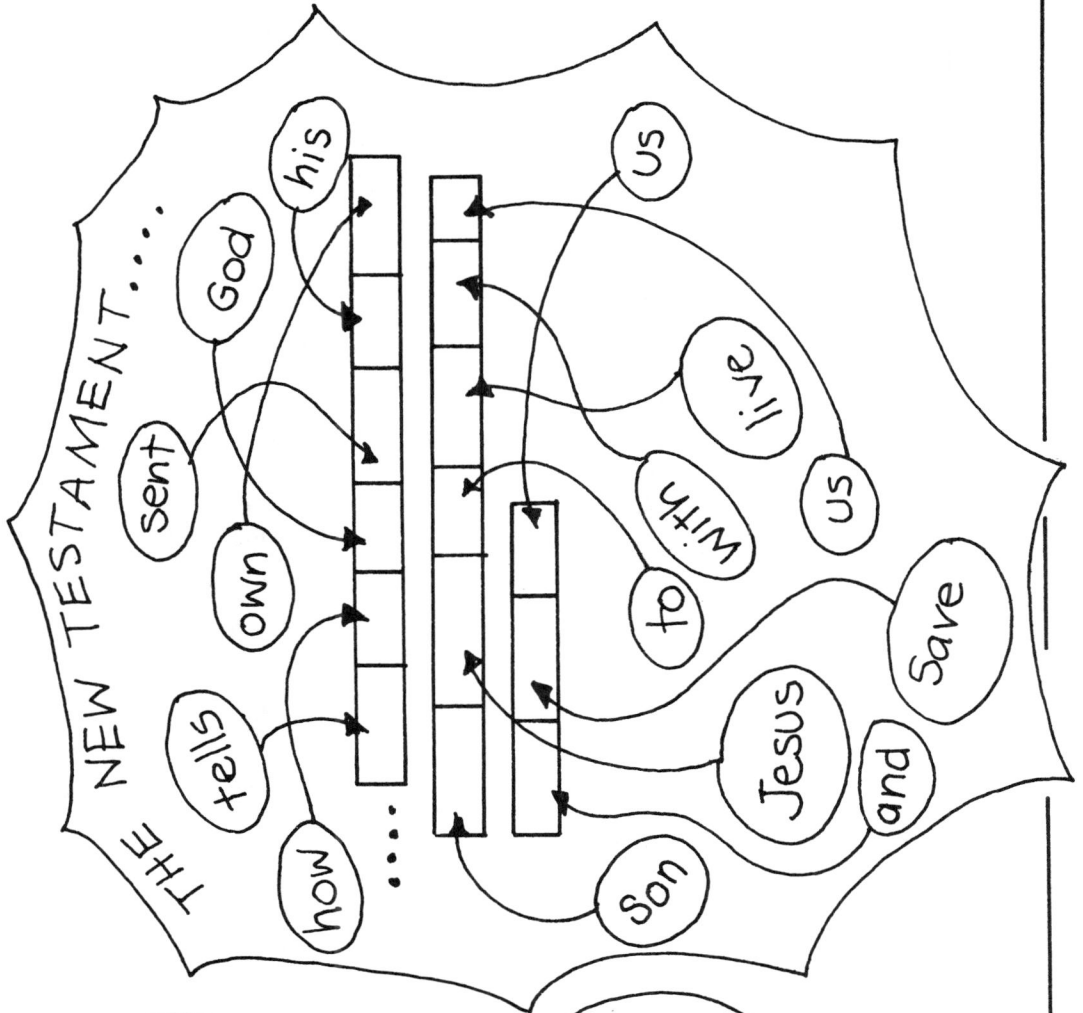

THE NEW TESTAMENT....

his
God
Sent
own
tells
how

us
live
with
us
to
Jesus
and
Save
Son

THE OLD TESTAMENT....

his
of
tells
and
people
God
how
the

led
love
his
to
the
made
world
us
know
ways

Mary will have a son and his name will be Jesus!

Matthew 1:18-23

The prophets said this child would be known as

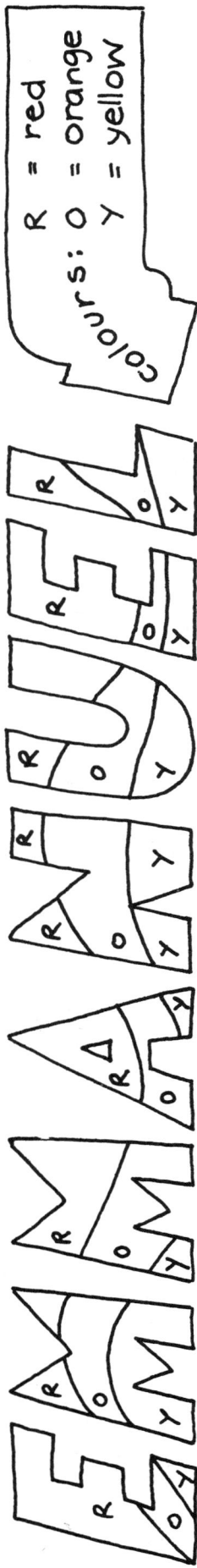

colours: R = red
O = orange
Y = yellow

EMMANUEL

which means

GOD WITH US

Jigsaw message!

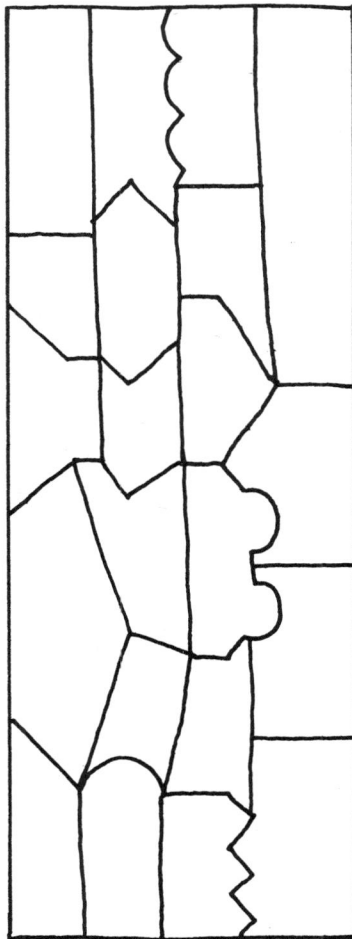

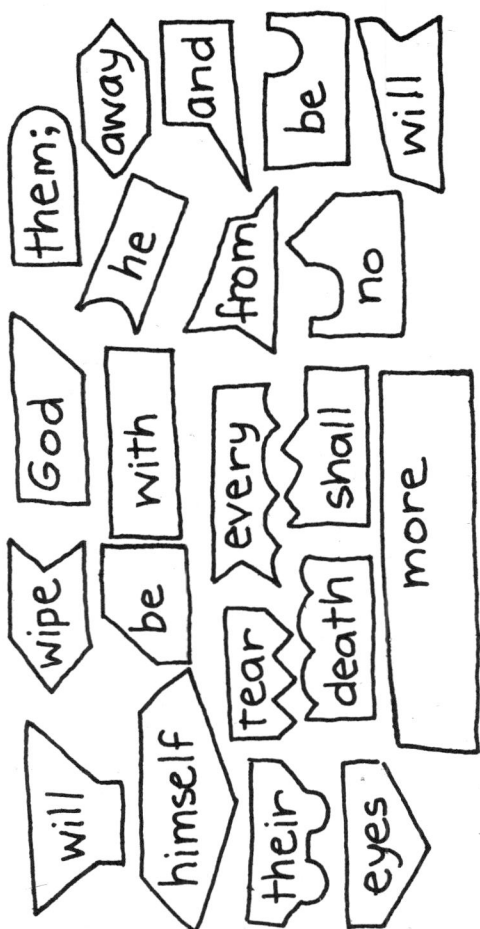

Revelation 21:1-7

them;
away
and
be
will

he
from
no

God
with
every
shall
death
more

wipe
be
tear

will
himself
their
eyes

"JUST AS YOU PROMISED, MY EYES HAVE SEEN THE ONE WHO WILL SAVE US."

Luke 2:22-40

This man's name is

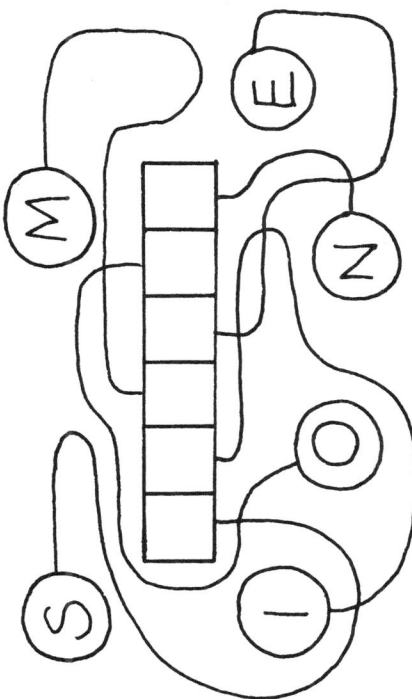

M E N O I S

He had hoped all his life to see the saviour of the world. And now......

THENIRECOGNISEDATJESUS SWASHTHERESAVIOURS

Colour the dotted letters.

What are these birds for?

PAIR

SON

SACRIFICE

PIGEONS

LORD

Every first born ---- was presented to the ----, and a ---- was offered, which was a ---- of turtle doves or ----.

THEY FOLLOWED THE STAR

AND FOUND JESUS.

Matthew 2:1-12, 19-23

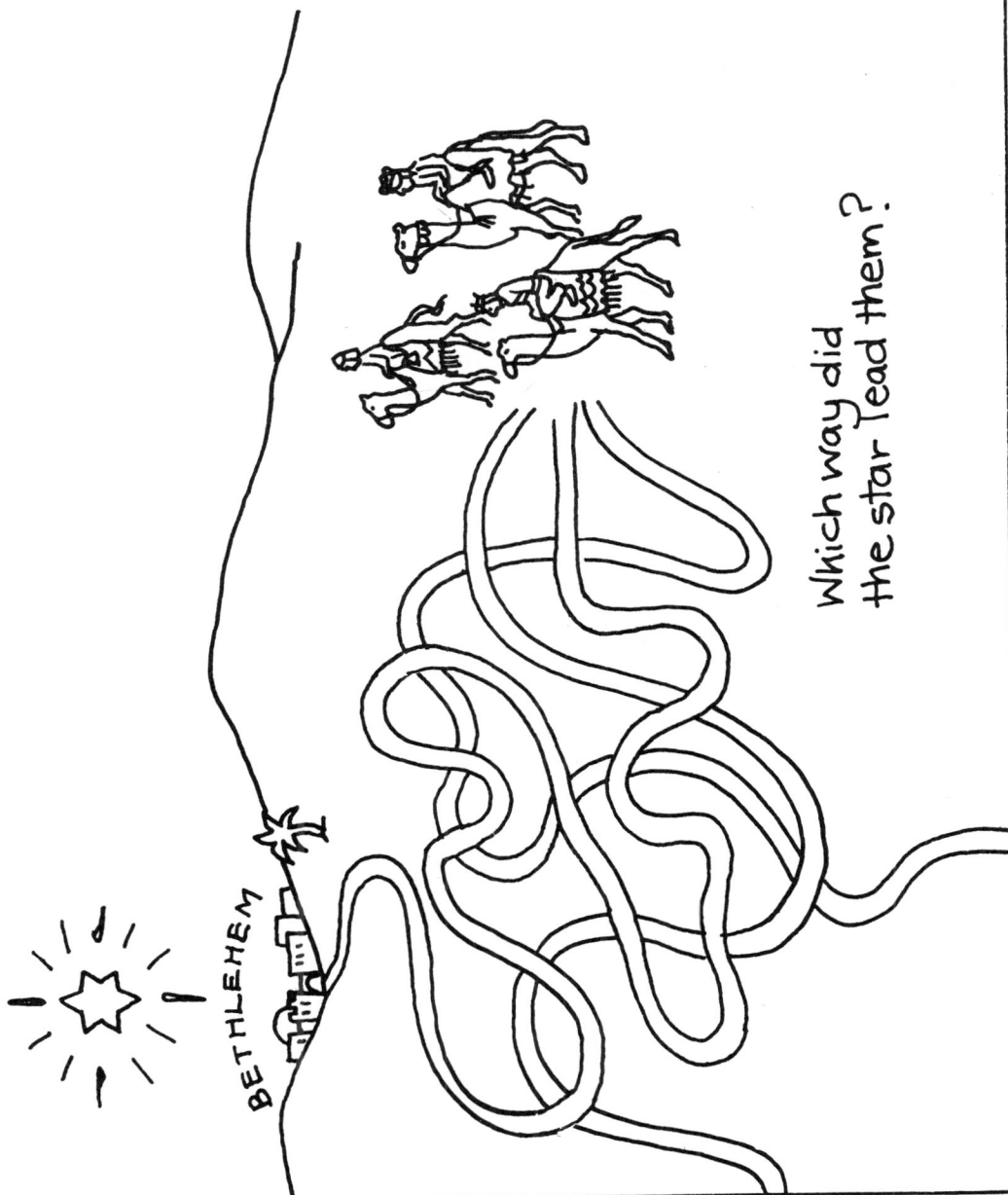

A	G	D	E	D	O	R	E	H	F	L	B
W	W	O	L	L	O	F	I	R	X	Q	F
O	B	R	R	O	D	S	D	R	E	A	M
L	W	C	P	A	G	K	H	Y	C	O	E
L	M	V	J	Y	T	T	E	M	E	N	H
O	Z	F	P	I	H	S	R	O	W	N	L
F	R	A	N	K	I	N	C	E	N	S	E
D	A	U	B	W	D	G	I	K	S	Y	J

GOLD   FOLLOW

FRANKINCENSE   STAR

MYRRH   HEROD

WISE   DREAM

MEN   WORSHIP

BETHLEHEM

Which way did
the star lead them?

Q. Why did John the Baptist duck people under the water?

A. As a

that their

were

away.

'HE IS THE CHOSEN ONE OF GOD.'

Isaiah 42:1-7 and John 1:29-34

Isaiah's Prophecy

My _____ _____ will not _____ a bruised _____ _____, or snuff out a smouldering _____. He will bring justice and light to all _____. He will open eyes _____ _____ and set captives _____ that are _____ _____ _____ _____

blind

reed

wick

break

people

servant

free

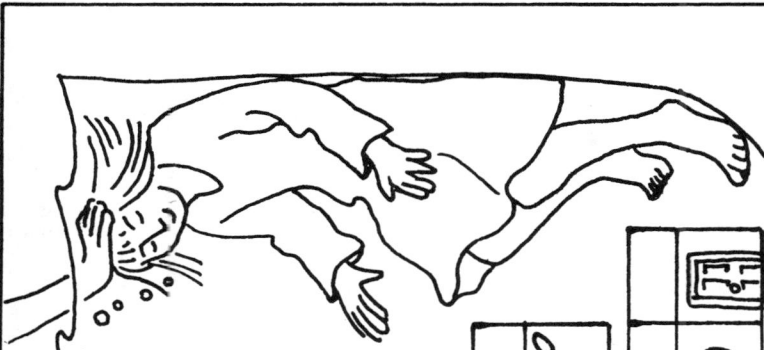

When Jesus was baptised, the Spirit came down from heaven. It looked like this.

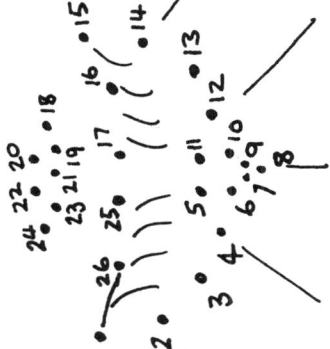

Jesus was . . . .

R

S

I

R

. . . . in God's glory

JESUS' FACE SHONE LIKE THE SUN.

Matthew 17:1-13

Join the dots to see what Moses can see

Then colour the picture   Exodus 3:1-6

NOTHING CAN SEPARATE US FROM GOD'S LOVE!

Romans 8:38-39

Q. Where did Jesus say he was going?

A. He said he was going

John 16:28

DEATH

LOVE

WILL

LIFE

FOR

LAST

THROUGH

AND

GOD'S

ME

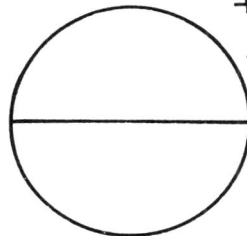
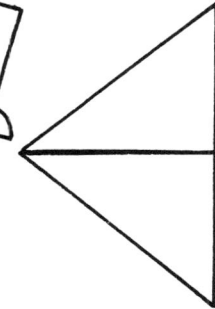
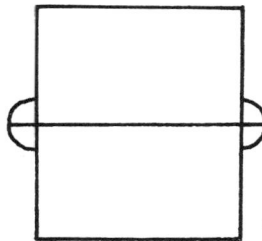
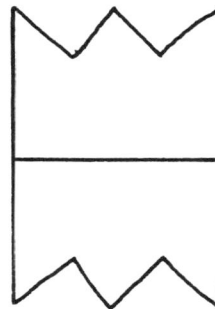

Put the shapes together and read the message

JESUS FEEDS 5000 PEOPLE.

John 6:1-14

START

find your
way
to the
bread and fish

Jesus showed his glory by this

HIS GNOMS
JEAN LORDS

colour the dotted letters.

Draw in the faces, then colour the picture.

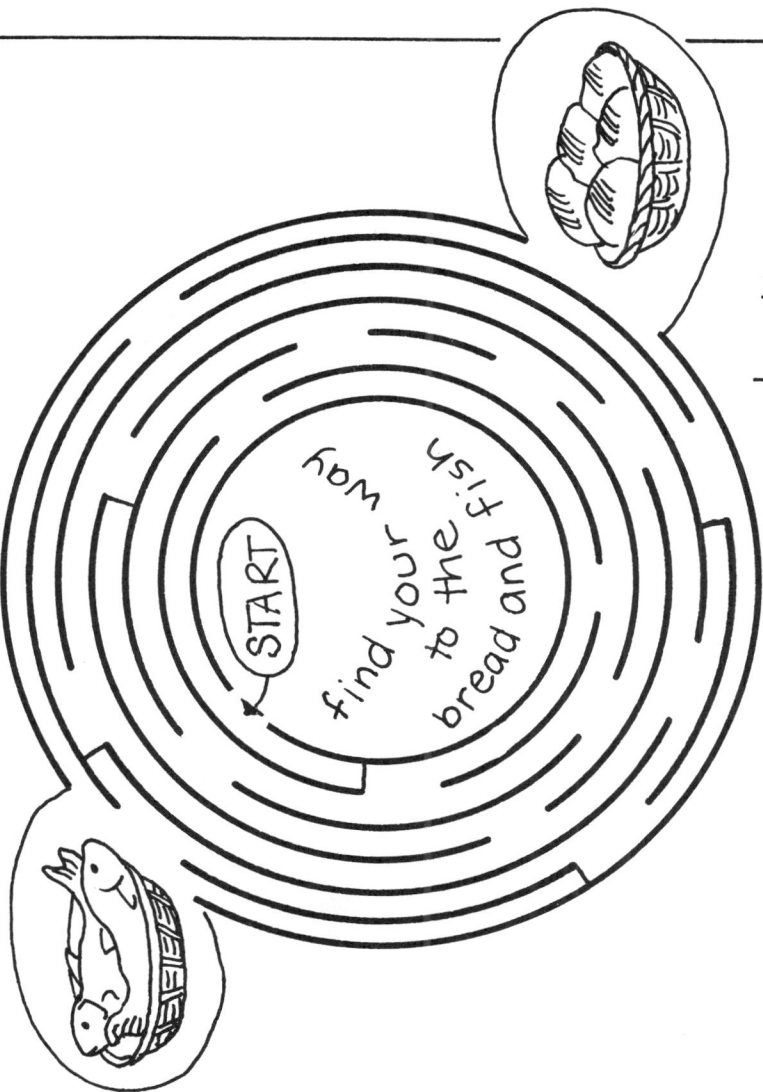

SOME SEED FELL INTO GOOD SOIL AND GREW.

What will these seeds grow into?

A	C	F	I	O	K	G	R	S	V
F	A	R	M	E	R	A	M	E	T
B	O	B	U	E	E	I	D	E	L
N	I	H	W	P	H	T	Z	D	N
Y	S	R	P	H	T	A	P	E	F
L	G	S	D	J	I	H	V	K	U
E	K	E	B	S	W	L	I	O	S
K	C	W	Y	J	Q	C	W	H	G
R	O	T	I	U	R	F	M	C	Q
S	R	D	T	H	O	R	N	S	X

FARMER WITHER BIRDS
SOW THORNS GREW
SEED CHOKED ROCK
PATH SOIL FRUIT

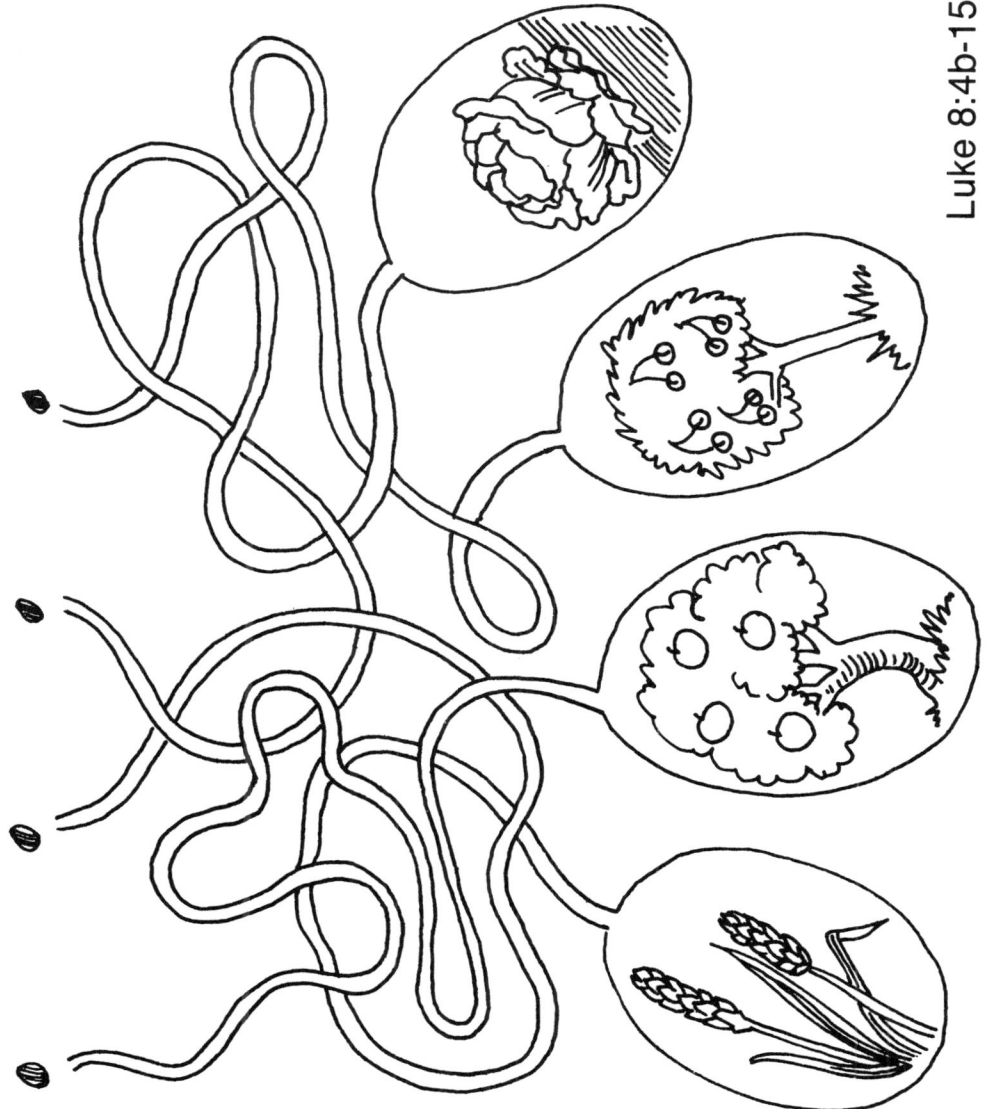

Luke 8:4b-15

HE EVEN MAKES THE DEAF HEAR AND THE DUMB SPEAK!

Mark 7:31-37

★ How did the deaf man get to Jesus?
(Cross out every BRING)

BRINGHIBRINGSBRINGFRIBRINGENDSBRING
BROUBRINGGHTBRINGHIMBRINGALBRINGONG.

★ Why did they bother?
(Cross out every FAITH)

THE FAITHYFAITHTRUSFAITHTEDFAITHTHAT
JEFAITHSUSFAITHWOFAITHULDFAITHHEFAITHLP.

A	E	I
B	G	J
D	H	N

Can you crack the code?

Luke 24:33-34

JESUS IS ALIVE!

EARLY on SUNDAY MORNING the WOMEN went to the TOMB. They found the STONE had been ROLLED AWAY. An ANGEL told them that JESUS was ALIVE again, just as he had PROMISED!   Mark 16:1-8

E	I	B	Q	R	O	L	L	E	D
F	A	E	J	E	S	U	S	X	Y
M	O	R	N	I	N	G	W	P	A
C	V	G	L	E	D	O	H	D	D
U	L	T	M	Y	V	C	T	H	N
Z	T	O	K	B	A	I	S	U
M	W	M	S	J	O	W	L	R	S
A	N	B	L	E	G	N	A	A	F
E	G	D	E	S	I	M	O	R	P

'I AM THE BREAD OF LIFE.'

John 6:32-40

The people didn't know what it was, so they called it MANNA, which means:

T ? I
W I T H A S

Exodus 16:2-15

well   as   Spirit   as our   body!

yum! yum!

BREAD

We need to feed our

When did you last eat BREAD? _____

When will you eat it again? _____

Why do you eat? _____

A	R	C	S	O	N	M	H	D	D
S	E	K	I	B	W	O	D	I	W
D	H	B	R	E	A	T	H	E	U
A	T	P	E	C	A	D	G	D	J
I	O	N	R	L	H	O	U	S	E
L	M	B	I	A	I	W	D	T	T
L	Q	V	J	B	Y	H	Q	H	K
N	Z	E	I	X	O	V	E	R	E
D	L	I	H	C	F	E	D	A	S
E	O	Y	G	R	E	U	M	W	P

The SON of a WIDOW got ILL and DIED. ELIJAH was staying at the HOUSE at the time. Elijah PRAYED and stretched himself OVER the child THREE times. The CHILD started to BREATHE again. Elijah brought him to his MOTHER, "Look," he said, "your son is ALIVE!"

1 Kings 17:17-end

JESUS SAID, "I AM THE RESURRECTION AND THE LIFE!"

John 11:17-27

LAZARUS IS BROUGHT TO LIFE

Q. Why did Jesus know someone had touched him so as to be healed?

GONE   HAD

HIM   HE   THAT

POWER   OUT   FELT

BECAUSE   OF

Luke 8:40-56

'YOUR FAITH HAS CURED YOU. GO IN PEACE.'

Luke 8:48

GIVE   MY   UP

GET   EAT   SPIRIT   CHILD

JAIRUS' DAUGHTER HAD DIED

Jesus said to her, " ◻ ♡ ◇ ". Her ◇ returned...and he told them to ⬭ her something to ◻

generous

kind
happy
gentle

AFTER

mean miserable
proud

unkind
selfish

BEFORE

IN CHRIST
YOU ARE
A NEW
PERSON!

2 Corinthians 5:17

1. What town was he in?
2. What was wrong with him?
3. What was his father's name?
4. What did Jesus say to him?

Mark 10:46-end

Colour in the right squares as you go.

Go! I can't help you

Go! your faith has cured you

Go! show yourself to a priest

Go! Come back tomorrow

Timaeus

Timothy

Thomas

4

Trevor

3

He couldn't talk

He was blind

He was deaf

He couldn't walk

2

Jerusalem

Nazareth

Jericho

Cana

1

Help Bartimaeus reach Jesus

Join the dots to see what God provided for the sacrifice in the end.

Genesis 22:1-18

Jigsaw message

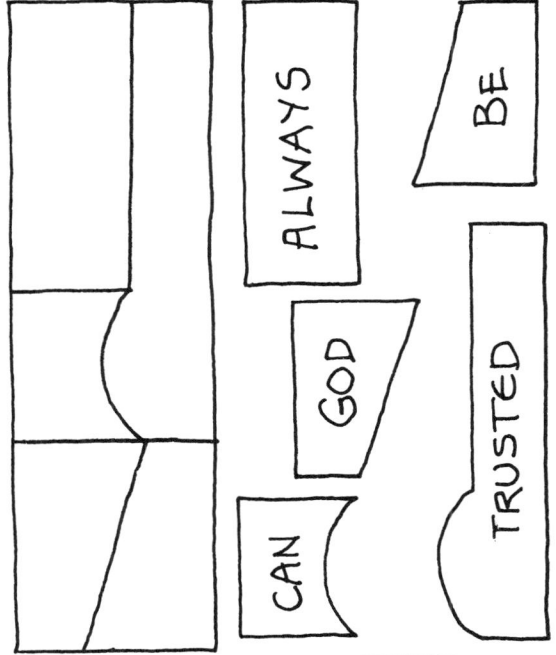

ALWAYS
BE
GOD
CAN
TRUSTED

GOD SAID TO ABRAHAM, 'NOW I KNOW THAT YOU TRUST ME!'

Which way to the hill for the sacrifice?

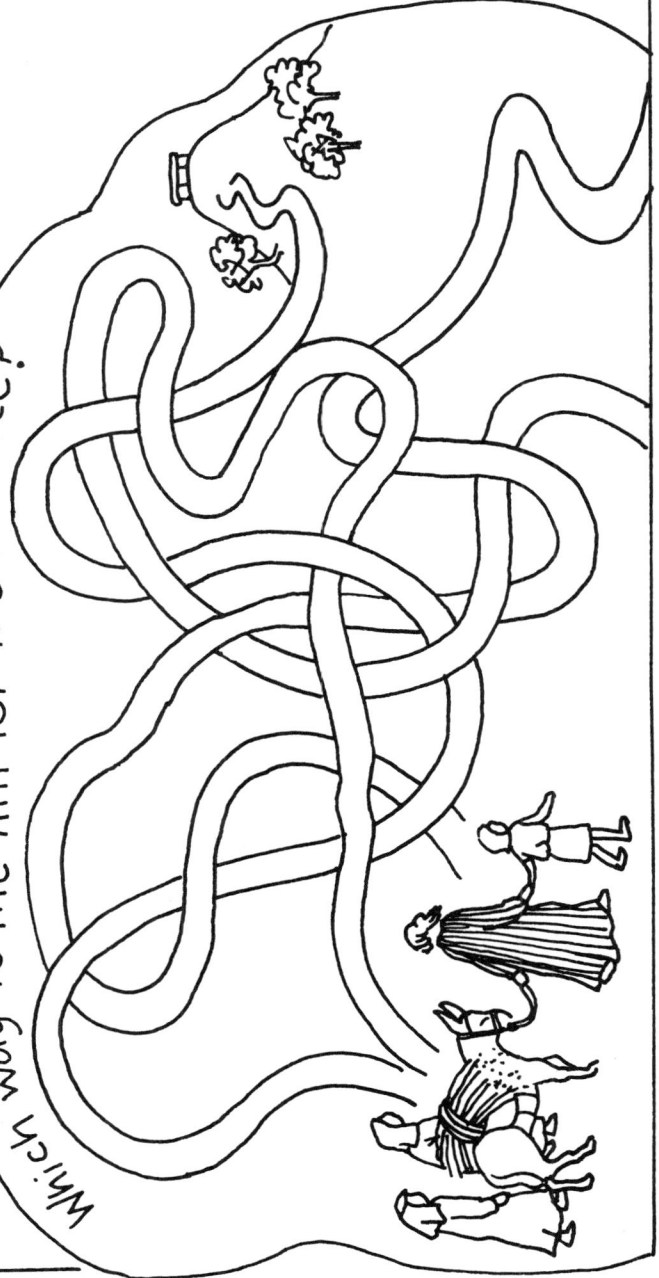

'YOU ARE MY PEOPLE?

I LOVE YOU!

Romans 9:19-26

How can you stay faithful?

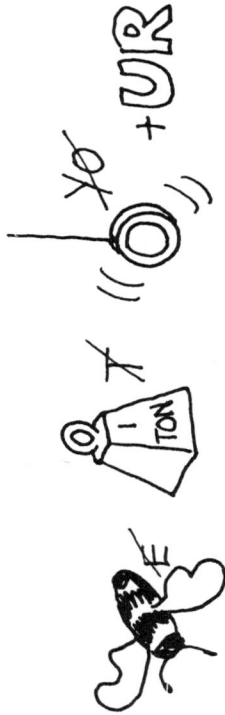

YO + UR

↑ TON

and stay close to Jesus

THIS WAY NOW

you made it ~ well done!

POSH WAY

PLEASE YOURSELF

DON'T BOTHER

COME IT ON

It is hard to stay faithful – try it!

FAME

THIS WAY

RICHES

1 John 3:1-10

KEY:

A	D	F	G	H	I	N	O	P	R
14	13	12	11	10	9	8	7	6	5

S	T	U	W
4	3	2	1

CRACK THE CODE TO READ THE MESSAGE

11,7,13 1,14,8,3,4 2,6 12,7,5 1,10,14,3 3,7

4,3,14,8,13 2,6 12,7,5 1,10,14,3 11,7,7,13

9,4 5,9,11,10,3 14,8,13 11,7,7,13

THOSE ON GOD'S SIDE ARE THOSE WHO DO WHAT IS RIGHT.

NOAH WAS ON GOD'S SIDE

Genesis 7:17-end

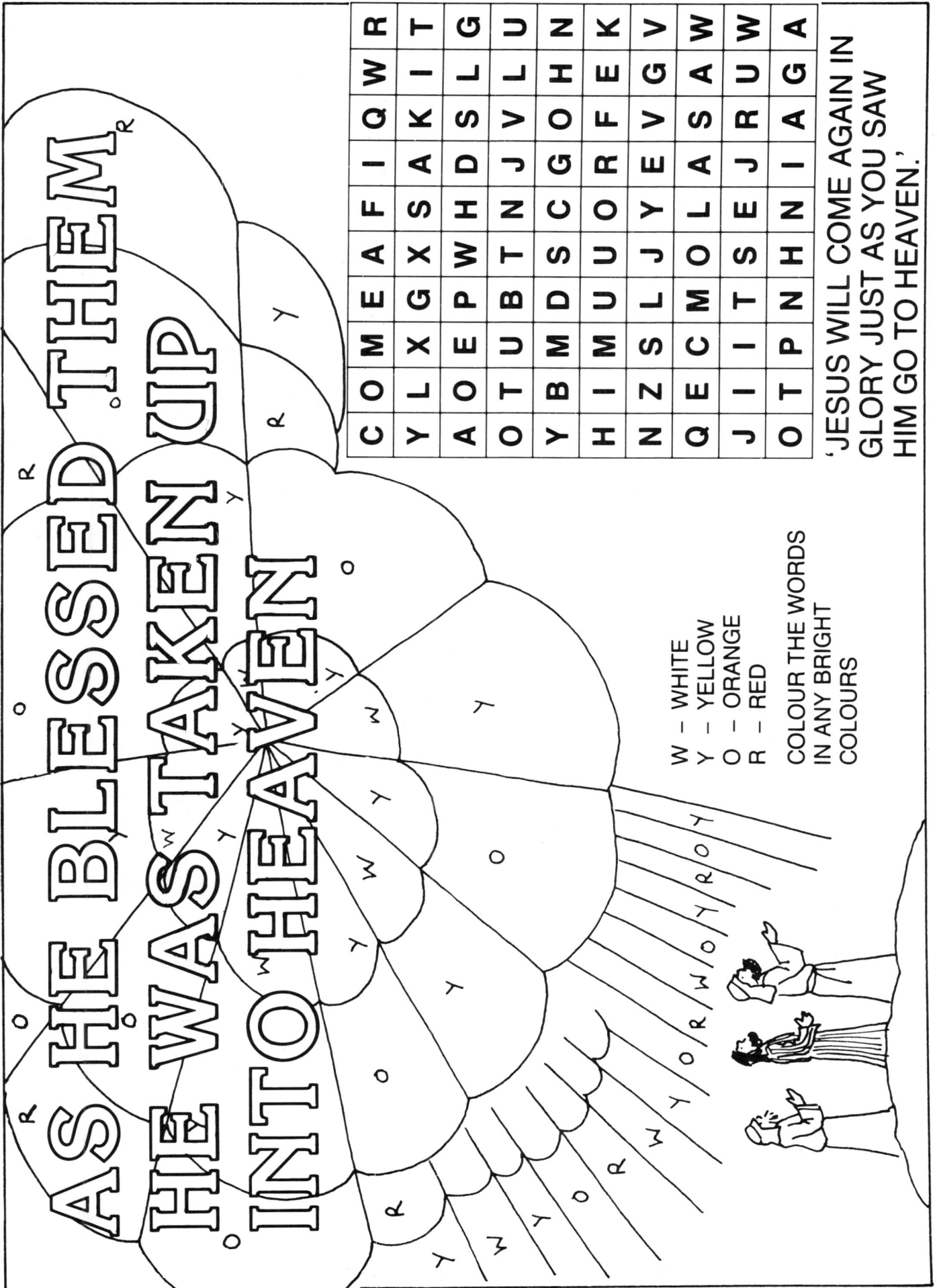

C	O	M	E	A	F	I	Q	W	R
Y	L	X	G	X	S	A	K	I	T
A	O	E	P	W	H	D	S	L	G
O	T	U	B	T	N	J	V	L	U
Y	B	M	D	S	C	G	O	H	H
H	I	M	U	U	O	R	F	E	K
N	Z	S	L	J	Y	E	V	G	V
Q	E	C	M	O	L	A	S	A	W
J	I	T	S	E	J	R	U	W	W
O	T	P	N	H	N	I	A	G	A

'JESUS WILL COME AGAIN IN GLORY JUST AS YOU SAW HIM GO TO HEAVEN.'

W – WHITE
Y – YELLOW
O – ORANGE
R – RED

COLOUR THE WORDS
IN ANY BRIGHT
COLOURS

AS HE BLESSED THEM
HE WAS TAKEN UP
INTO HEAVEN

FIX YOUR HOPES ON CHRIST JESUS.

1 Peter 1:13 and John 11:17-27

Jesus says,

What do we hope to share?

Romans 5:2, 5

Colour in the dotted letters

The serpent said to Eve

ABCDEFGHIKLNORSTUWY

But they weren't

Q. Who put things right?

A.

Colour the dotted letters   Genesis 3:1-15.

ADAM AND EVE DISOBEY GOD.

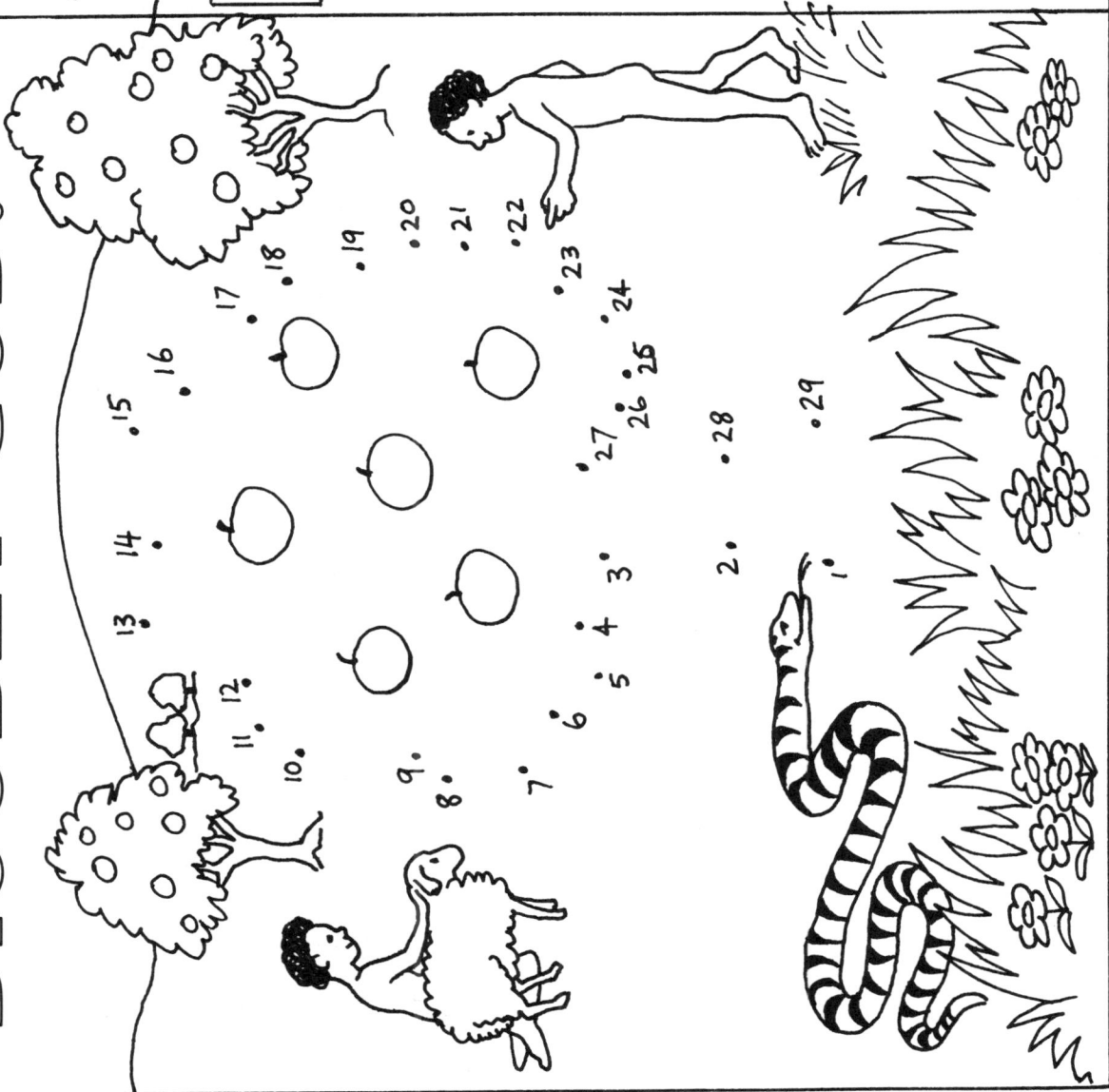

Jigsaw Message
1 Find the shape that fits
2 Write in the word on the person

very

is

and

do

difficult

what

all

good

find

it

right

to

we

Jesus Christ

is the friend of sinners

Colossians 1:18-23

5 he

2 knows

8 us

9 !

6 still

4 and

7 loves

1 God

3 this

IF YOU ARE THE SON OF GOD

○ ○ ○ ○ Luke 4:1-13

WANTED FOR MURDER

A N
I C
A

O

O

Draw him here

FOR THE MURDER OF

MOTIVE?

U A
E
Y
J S
O
L

A
E
L
B

Genesis 4:1-10

What happened in the wilderness?

Jesus was

2ⁿ  ø mp

e his

ø
P

in the ø wr

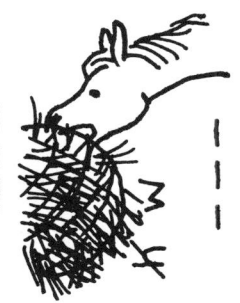
W
Y

ACT LIKE CHRIST, WITH FORGIVENESS AND CARING LOVE.

Galatians 6:1-5

Luke 7:36-end

1 Samuel 24:1-7

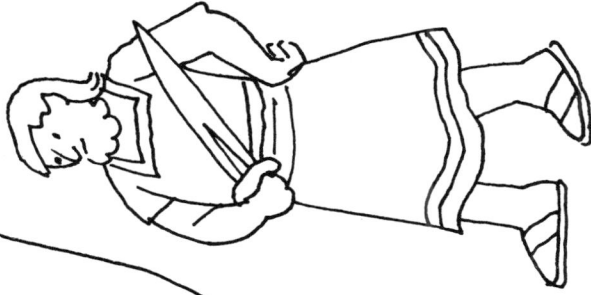

King Saul has been looking for David to kill him. Now David has the chance to kill Saul. What does he do?

Cuts off a bit of Saul's cloak but does no harm to Saul

Lets Saul go away without knowing his danger

Kills Saul in revenge

YES

NO

NO

Two men are let off a debt. One owed 50p the other £500. Which one will be most grateful?

ooo

If you're forgiven a lot, you'll love God a lot

'I AM SENDING MY MESSENGER
WHO WILL CLEAR A PATH
BEFORE ME'

Malachi 3:1-5
and Matthew 11:2-15

How can we prepare for Jesus? Write them in the stones

talking to God

being open-minded

forgiving

loving

reading the Bible

saying sorry

listening to God

thanking

Join the dots, then colour the picture

HERE I AM, LORD!

1 Samuel 3:1-10

SAMUEL was ASLEEP in the
TEMPLE when he heard someone
CALLING his NAME. He thought it
was ELI the PRIEST. THREE times
the VOICE came, so Eli realised
that GOD was calling Samuel. Next
time God called, Samuel
ANSWERED, 'Speak, Lord, I am
LISTENING.'

S	A	M	U	E	L	B	C	A
G	D	I	K	E	I	C	T	N
O	P	E	E	L	S	A	S	S
D	H	R	F	M	T	L	E	W
N	H	E	L	E	E	L	I	E
T	O	G	M	J	N	I	R	R
S	R	P	T	A	I	N	P	E
U	L	V	Q	C	N	G	P	D
E	C	I	O	V	G	W	D	Y

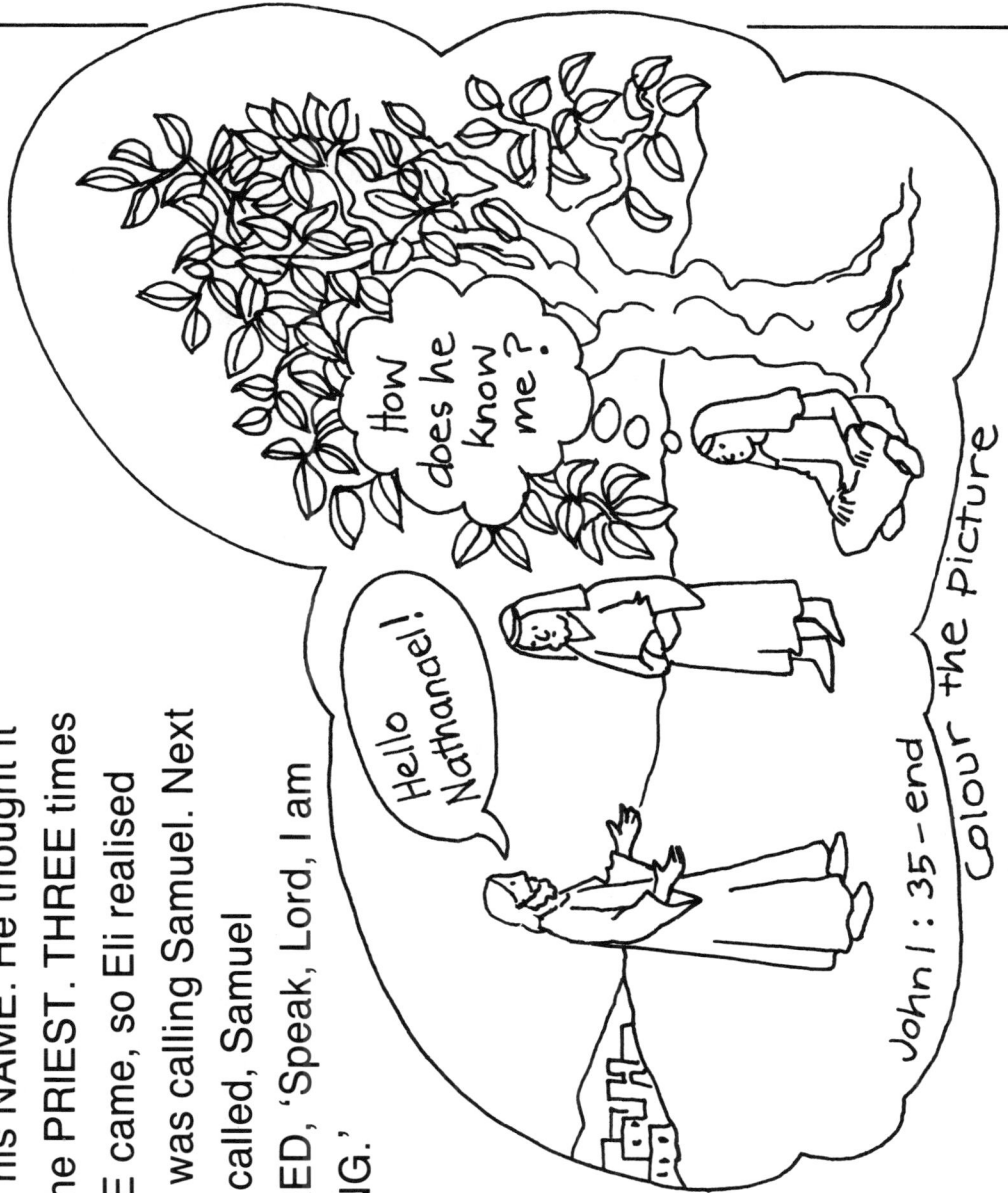

How does he know me?

Hello Nathanael!

John 1 : 35 – end

Colour the Picture

Cross out
every EAR to
read the
message!

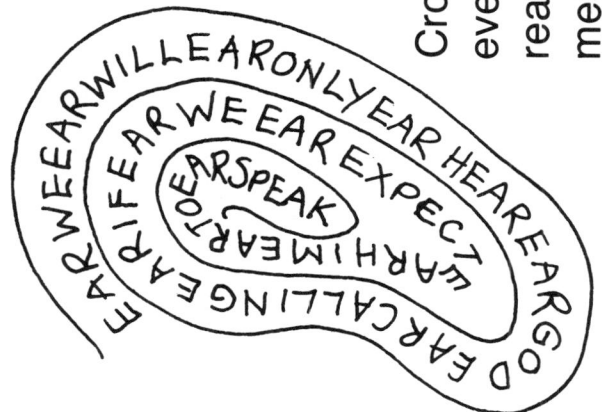

EARWEEARWILLEARONLYEARHEAREARGO
DEARCALLINGEARIFEARWEEAREXPECT
EARWEEARWEARHIMEARTO
EARSPEAK

WE MUST WORSHIP GOD IN SPIRIT AND TRUTH. John 4:19-26

Whatever we worship, God wants us to

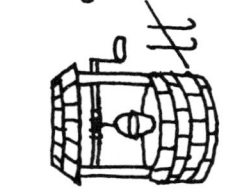

W

to
$

to
m
y
re

John 4:23-24

Why isn't God pleased with their worship?
The Sabbath day

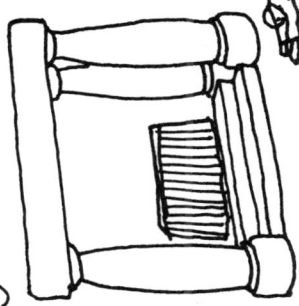

Monday, Tuesday, Wednesday, Thursday.....

Jeremiah 7:3-11

'TAKE UP YOUR CROSS AND FOLLOW ME.'

Matthew 16:24-28

  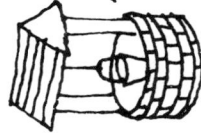 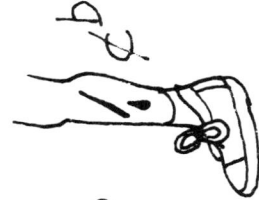 

Jesus   us to   what

Jesus   st up   is   and

is   Sometimes that

be   will   with   Jesus

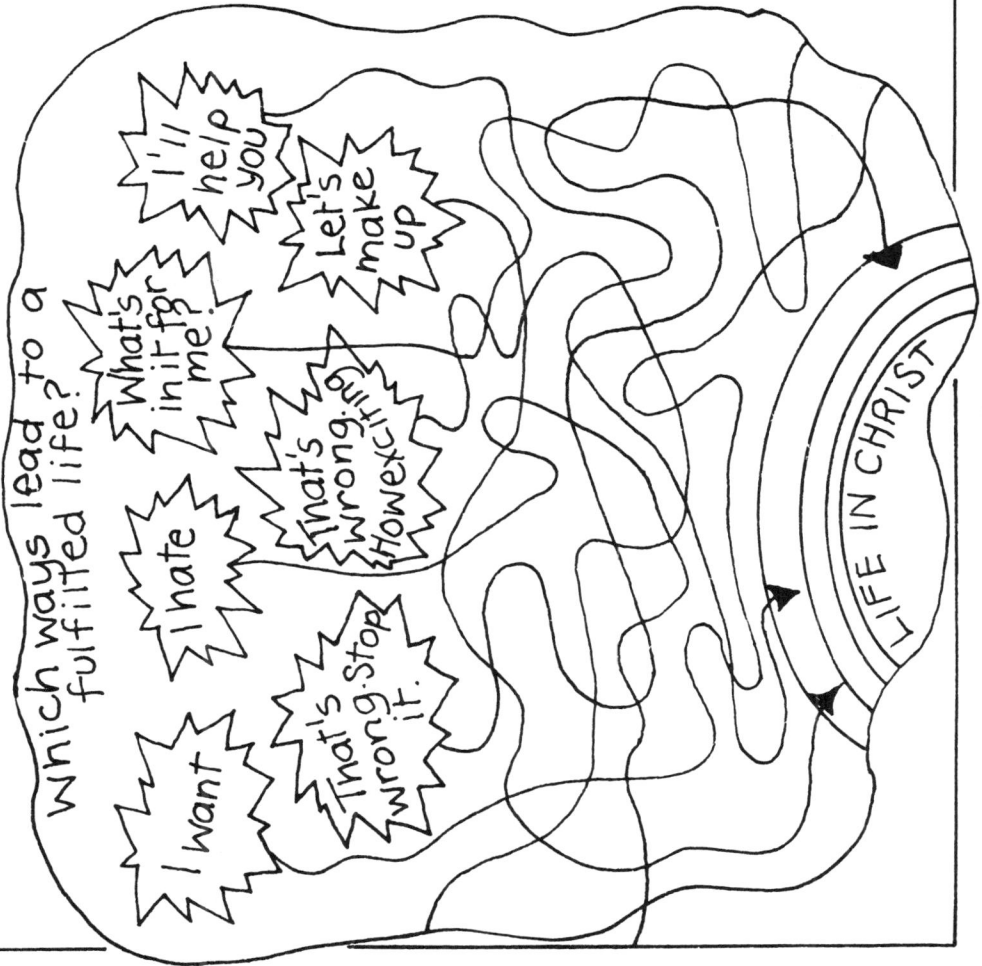

I'll help you

Let's make up

Which ways lead to a fulfilled life?

What's in it for me.

That's wrong. How exciting.

I hate

I want

That's wrong. Stop it.

LIFE IN CHRIST

* What makes a good shepherd?
(Cross out the things that don't)

STRONG
RELIABLE
WATCHFUL
GREEDY
CARELESS
SELFISH
CRUEL
BRAVE
LAZY
CARING
KIND

JESUS SAID, "I AM THE GOOD SHEPHERD."

John 10:7-16

Join the dots to make the picture

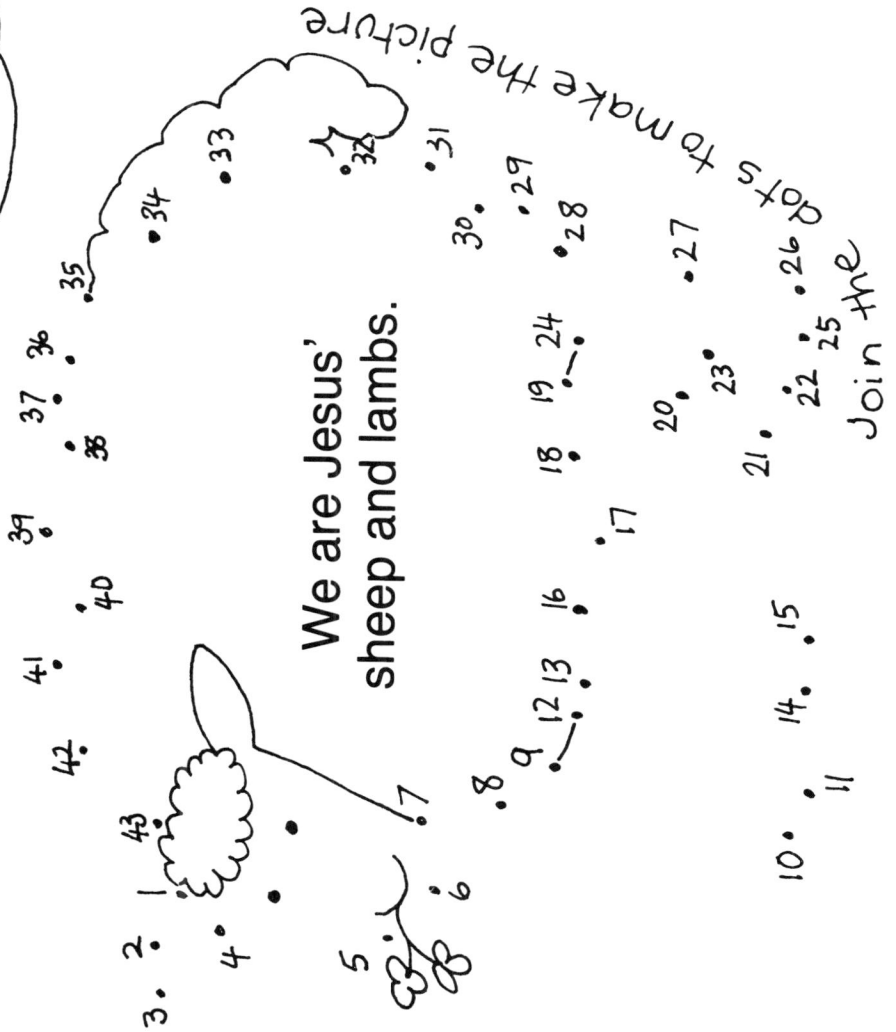

We are Jesus' sheep and lambs.

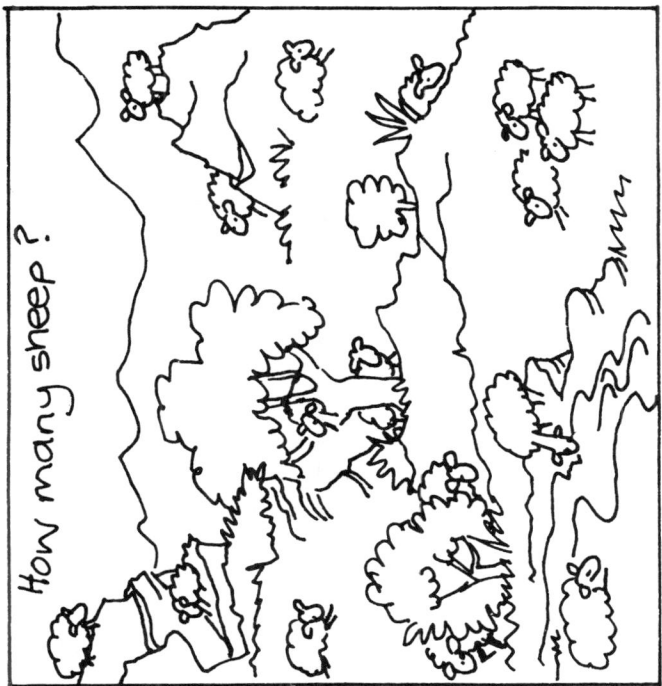

How many sheep?

There are sixteen sheep

IF YOU WANT TO BE GREAT, BE A SERVANT!

Mark 10:42-45

Sounds odd, doesn't it!
BUT...

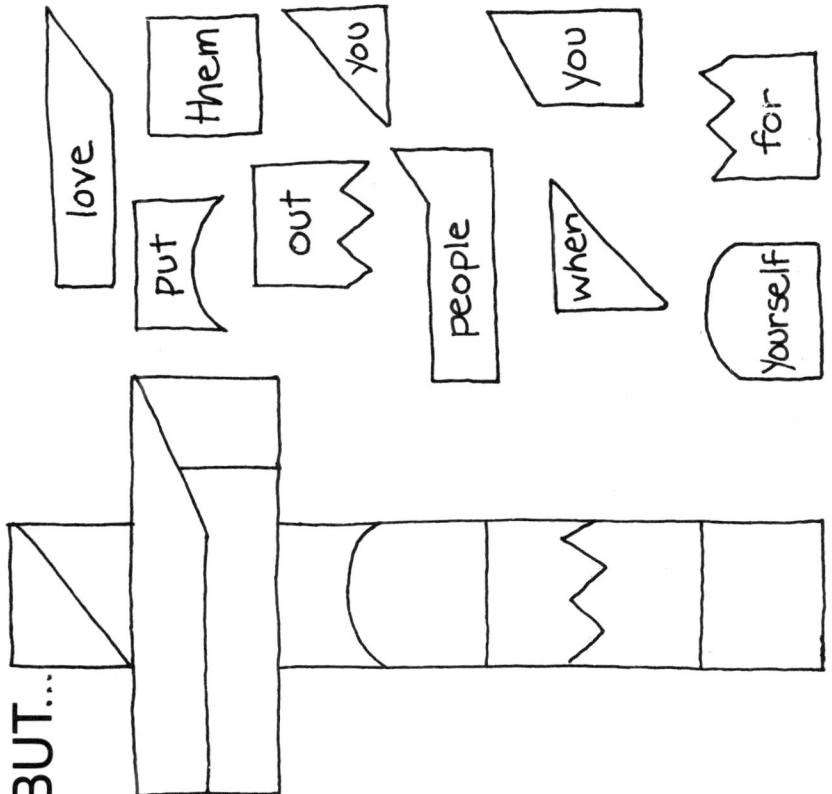

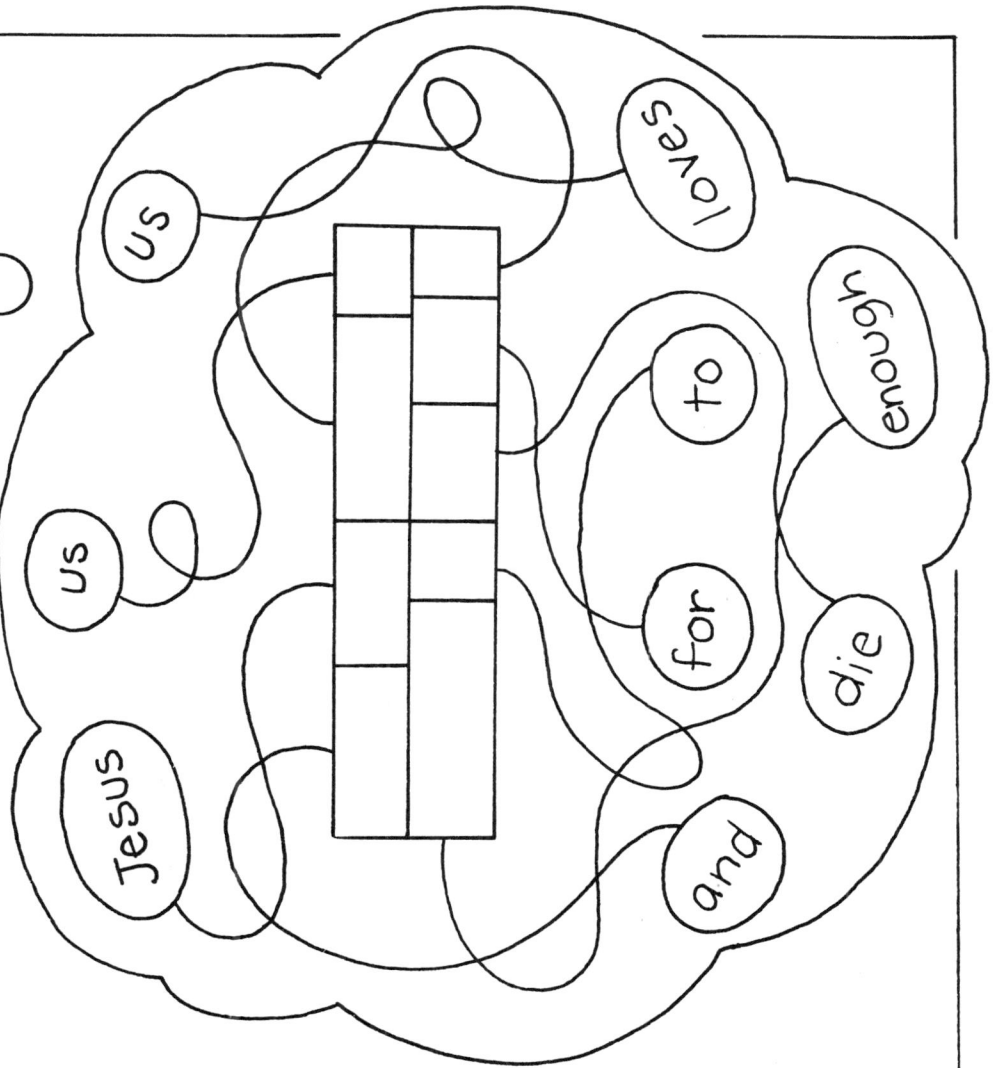

us

loves

us

enough

to

Jesus

die

for

and

love

them

you

you

put

out

for

people

when

yourself

JESUS SAID, 'I AM THE WAY, THE TRUTH AND THE LIFE.'

John 14:1-6

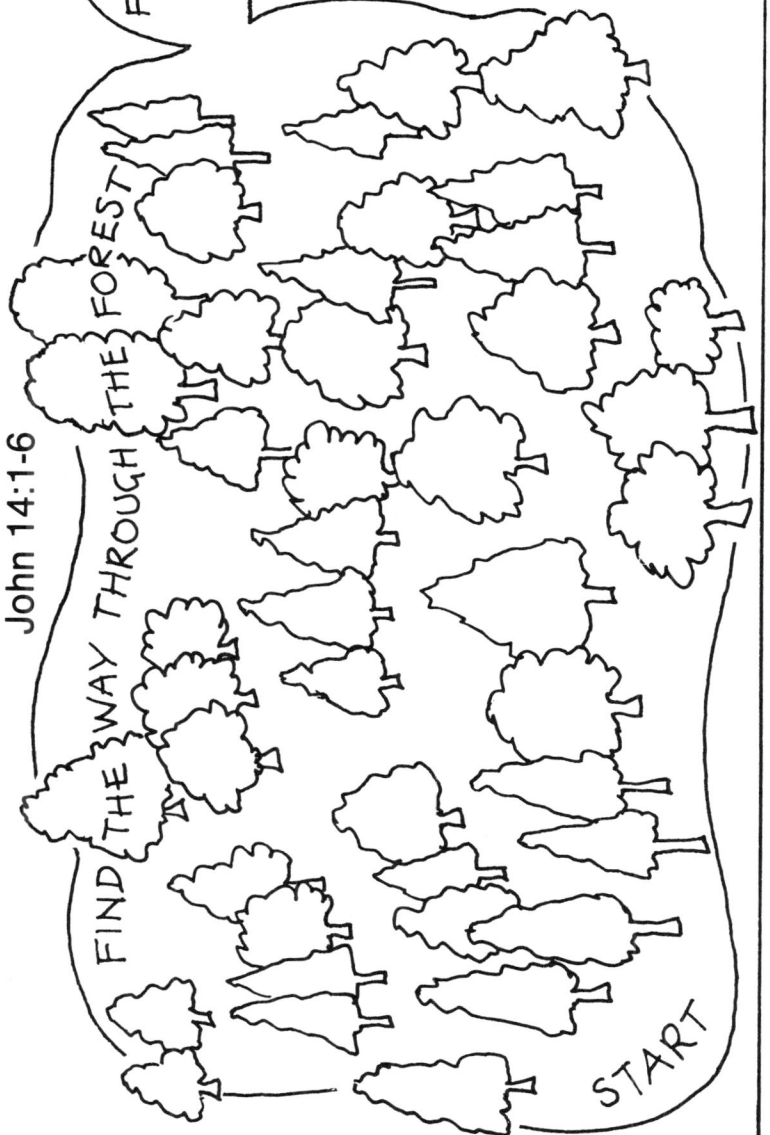

FIND THE WAY THROUGH THE FOREST

START

FINISH

THIS WAY
THIS WAY
THIS WAY
THIS WAY
THIS WAY

If we   the

2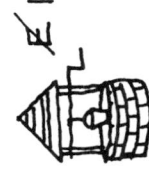

Jesus, he  show

us the way.

THEY WERE ALL FILLED WITH THE HOLY SPIRIT

Acts 2:1-4

COLOUR THE FLAMES

Red Yellow Yellow orange Yellow Red Orange Orange Red Yellow Orange Yellow Orange

The Holy Spirit fills us with this:

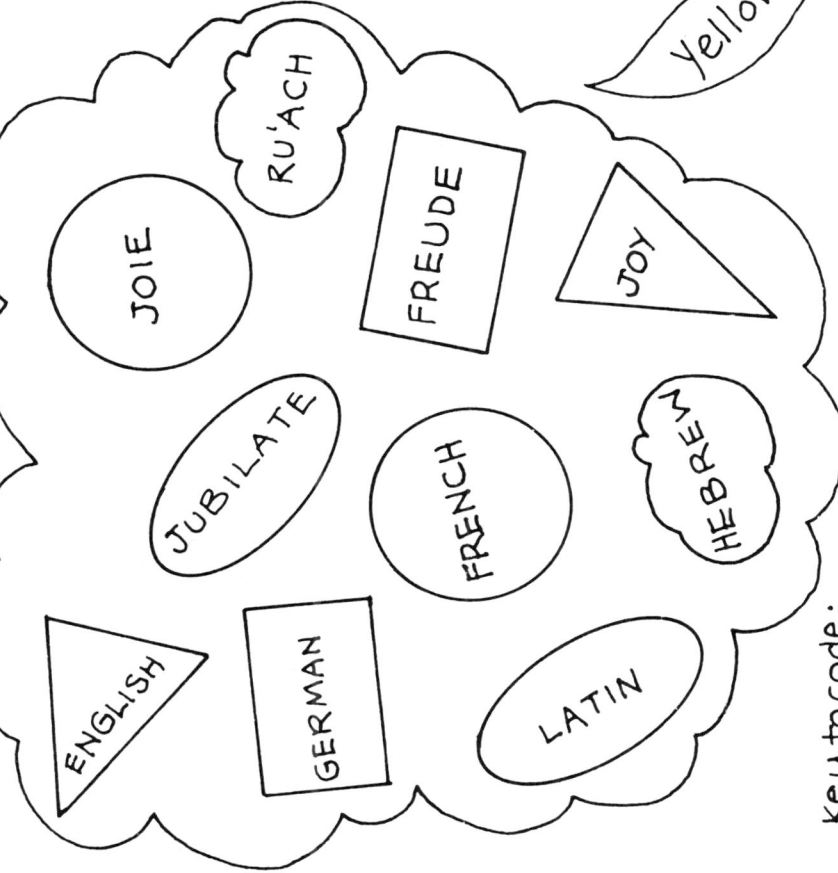

JOIE

RU'ACH

FREUDE

JOY

JUBILATE

FRENCH

HEBREW

ENGLISH

GERMAN

LATIN

Genesis 11:1-9

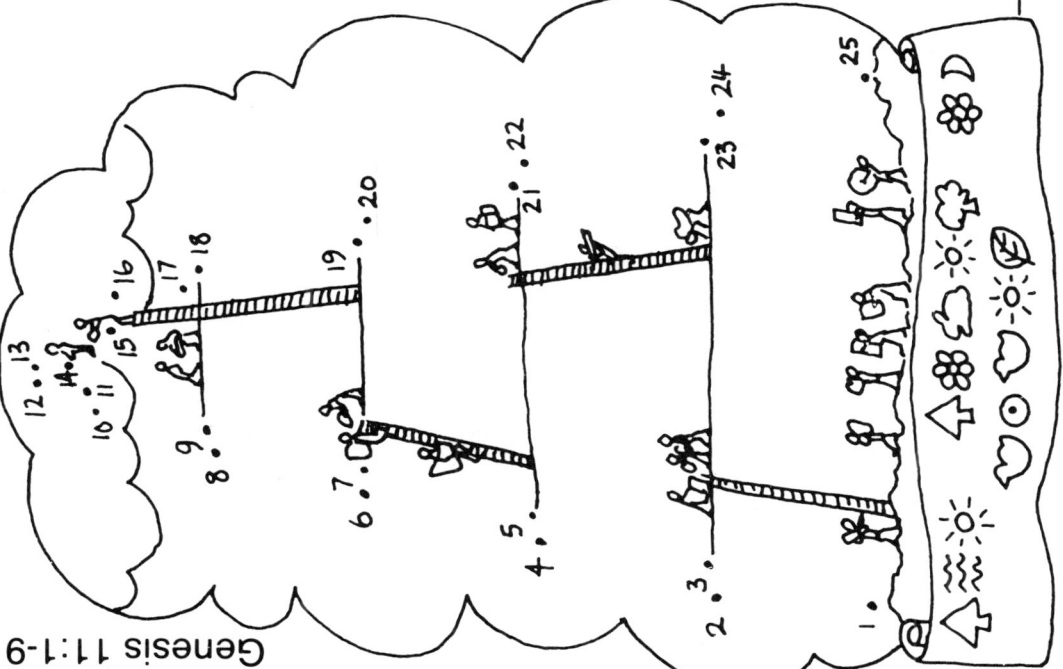

Key to code:

A	B	E	F	H	L	O	R	T	W
⊙	☁	☀	☽	≈	🌿	🌸	🍃	🌿	🐦

D	N	B	D	E	L	P	P	I	R	C
C	O	B	A	N	Q	U	E	T	A	D
S	N	O	I	T	A	T	I	V	N	I
E	E	A	N	G	R	Y	J	I	K	M
R	E	H	X	F	O	E	L	N	Y	S
V	O	H	Q	G	W	B	T	I	E	L
A	D	O	C	L	E	E	T	S	A	T
N	G	U	L	P	M	U	V	A	F	
T	U	S	R	U	E	C	A	B	L	M
S	Z	E	T	F	X	S	R	L	A	H
D	I	N	N	E	R	P	A	R	T	Y

One day a man gave a DINNER PARTY. He sent out INVITATIONS but the people he had invited ALL made EXCUSES. The MASTER of the house was ANGRY and told his SERVANTS to go and bring in the POOR, the CRIPPLED, the LAME and the BLIND. "I want my HOUSE to be FULL," he said. "NONE of those invited will TASTE my BANQUET."   Luke 14:15-24

THEY SHARED THEIR MEALS IN LOVE AND JOY

Acts 2:42-47

Snapshots of the early church
Draw in the pictures

They broke bread together

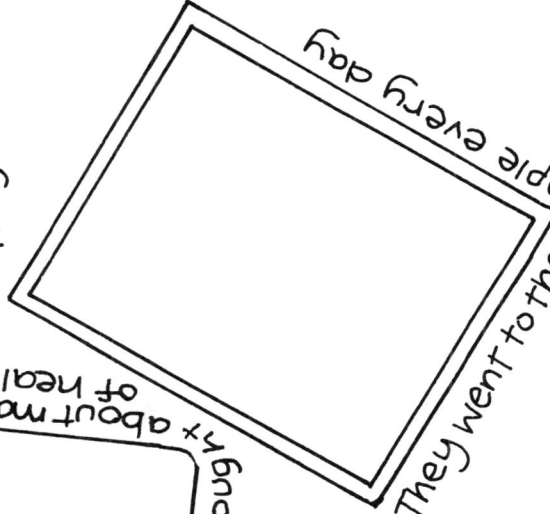

They went to the temple every day

The apostles brought about many miracles of healing

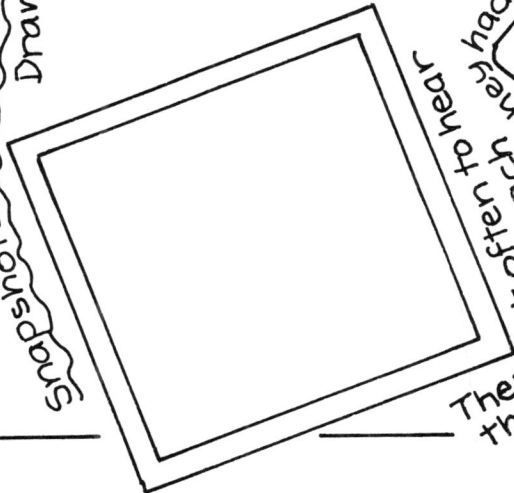

They met often to hear the apostles teach

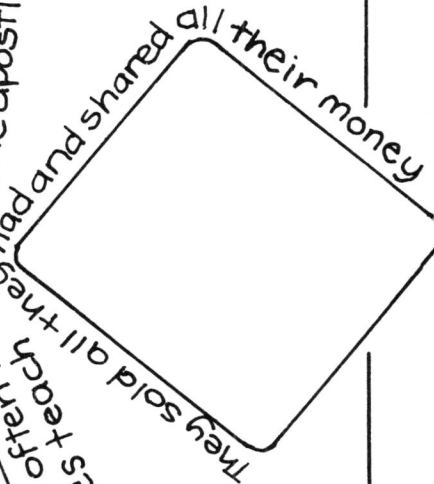

They sold all that they had and shared all their money

Help the shepherd find his sheep

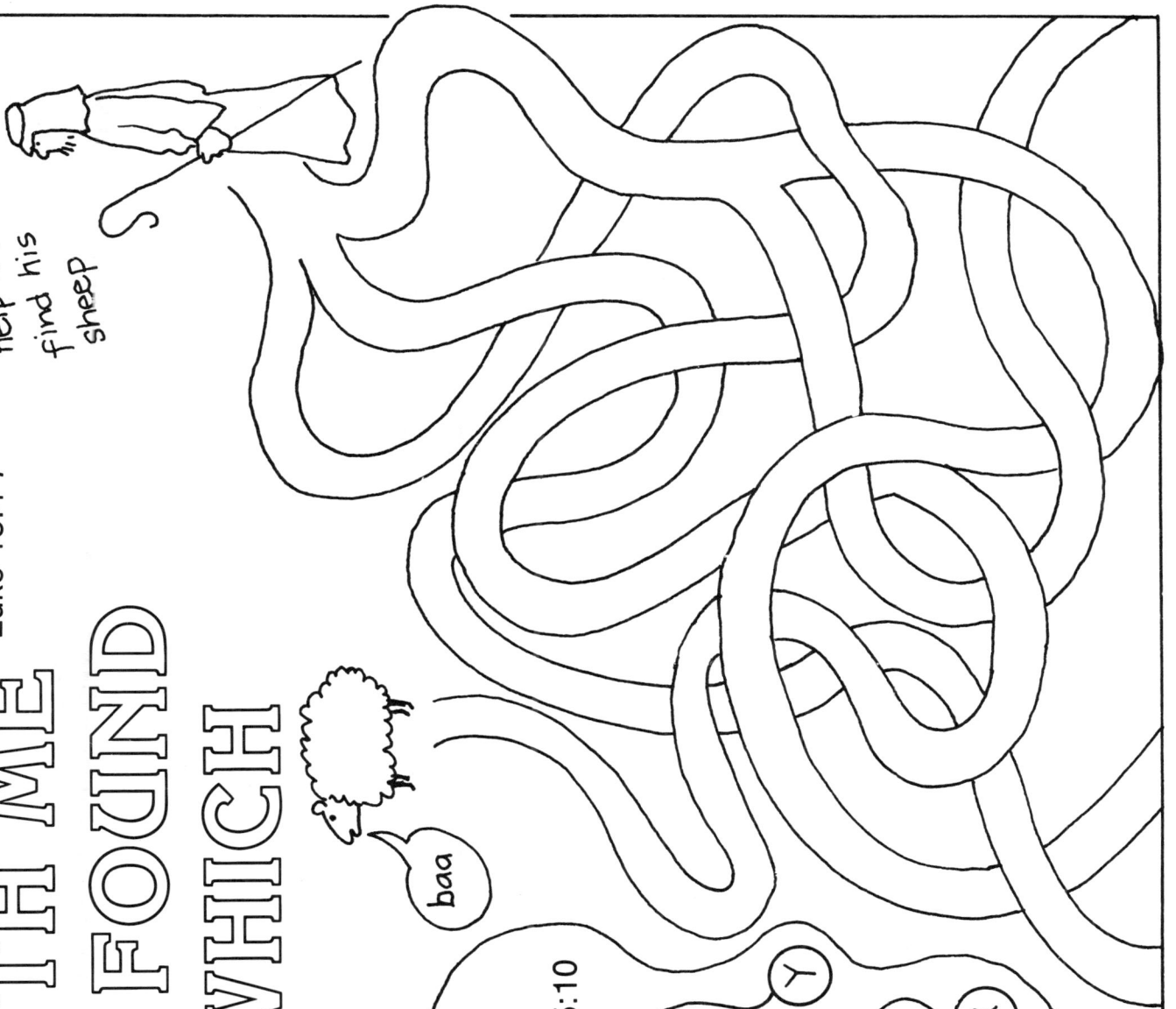

Luke 15:4-7

REJOICE WITH ME FOR I HAVE FOUND MY SHEEP WHICH WAS LOST!

baa

Q. Which people are most important to God?

Luke 15:10

A.

V Y R N E O E S P R E

GOD'S GOOD NEWS IS FOR EVERYONE.

Matthew 28:19

A GENTILE is anyone who is not a JEW.
Q. What did Peter find out at Caesarea?
A.

on Gentiles was and Jews Spirit that both Poured God's out

Jesus chose another out and tell everyone about God's kingdom.

by 18 ÷ 9 = to heal the sick He sent them

12 x 6 =

14 ÷ 7 =

people.

Luke 10:1-12

Acts 11:4-18

LOVING IS THE BEST WAY TO LIVE.

Mark 12:28-34

If you live by God's way of LOVE, what would you do about......

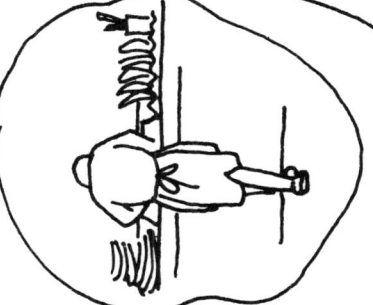

this?

this?

this?

this?

this?

Jesus sums up the law like this:

① ...L the ...L your God ...s ...L with your ♥ and ...L ...E+th ...ow and M... and

② ...L your ...A ou ...R as

LOVE YOUR ENEMIES; DO GOOD TO THOSE WHO WHO HATE YOU.

Luke 6:27-38

When God lives in us, it shows, and the world turns upside down!

treat them with kindness and pray for them

You must not curse them back. Bless them instead

offer him your shirt as well!

then willingly go 2 miles

If someone treats you spitefully.

If it someone curses you,

If a man takes your coat!

If you are forced to go one mile

MATCH THE PATCH

Can you see God's message? Colour it in, so it shows up clearly)

Ezekiel 37:1-14

LET THE MIND OF CHRIST
BE IN YOU IN THE WAY YOU
THINK AND LIVE.

Philippians 2:1-11

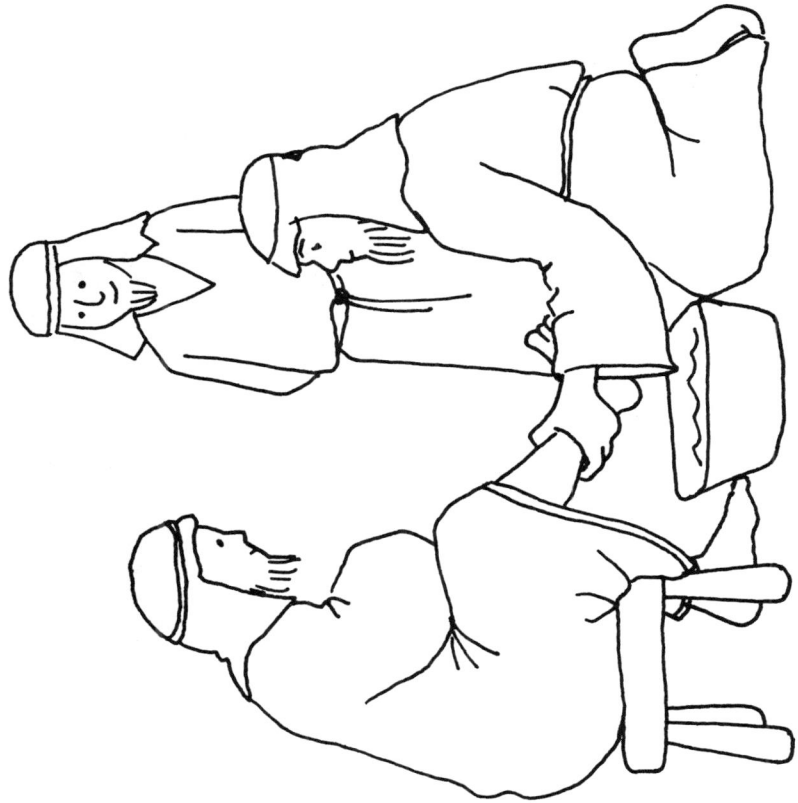

T	B	H	T	C	V	D	S	R	F
G	R	E	A	T	Q	D	H	T	O
X	E	E	W	C	O	I	U	N	L
F	B	Z	A	G	U	S	M	A	L
B	P	N	E	T	H	C	I	V	O
Y	E	V	A	O	D	I	L	R	W
H	O	E	W	F	M	P	I	E	E
L	J	E	S	U	S	L	T	S	R
F	D	L	O	R	D	E	Y	E	S
O	J	G	D	E	H	S	A	W	T

When Jesus WASHED the FEET of his
DISCIPLES, he SHOWED them how they were to
TREAT one another. JESUS was their LORD, but
he acted as their SERVANT. So if his FOLLOWERS
want to be GREAT in GOD'S EYES they must look
after one another with LOVE and HUMILITY.

John 13:1-15

Who is willing to give to the Lord today?

EAM
E L B R

O D B Z
R E N

R O
N

O D
G L

E W E
J S L

S R L V
L E

Solomon is collecting materials for building a beautiful temple. What are the people bringing?

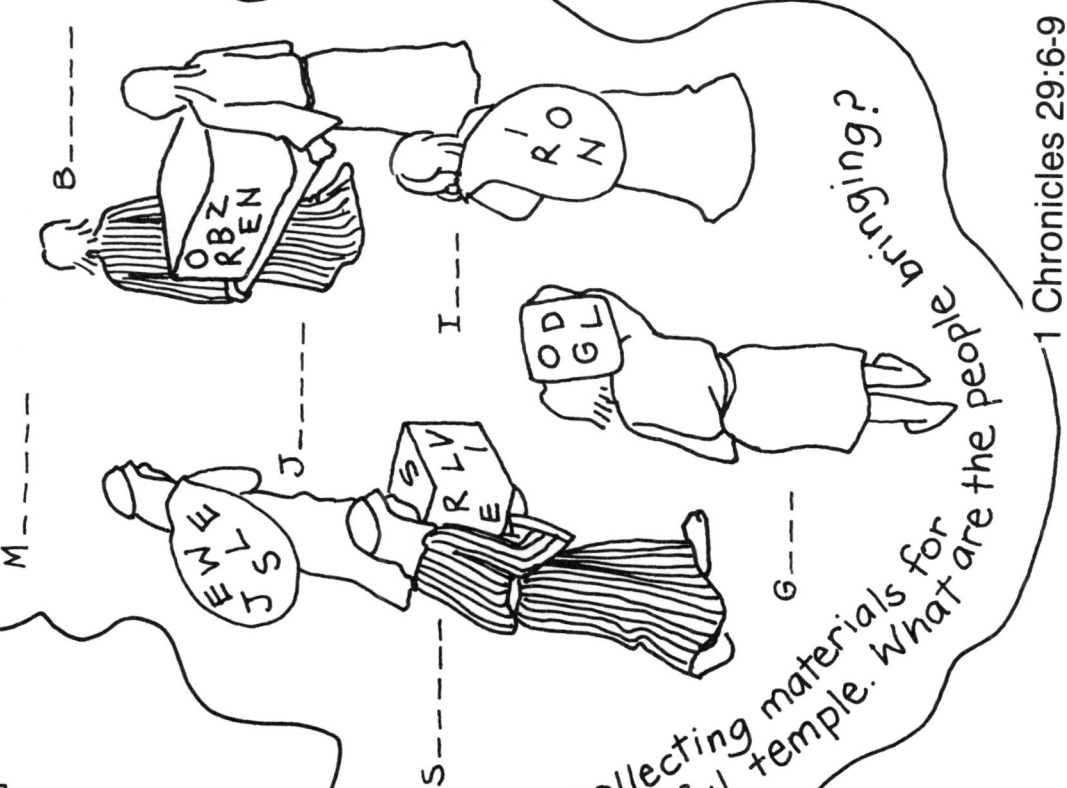

1 Chronicles 29:6-9

ENCOURAGE ONE ANOTHER AS YOU WORK TOGETHER.

Philippians 1:1-11

How are these people working with Christ?

A doctor?

A farmer?

A scientist?

An artist?

You?

Draw them at work

'Let your life shine to show God's glory!'

red
red
red
red
red
red
red
orange
yellow

WE WILL WALK
IN THE NAME
OF THE LORD
OUR GOD! Micah 4:5

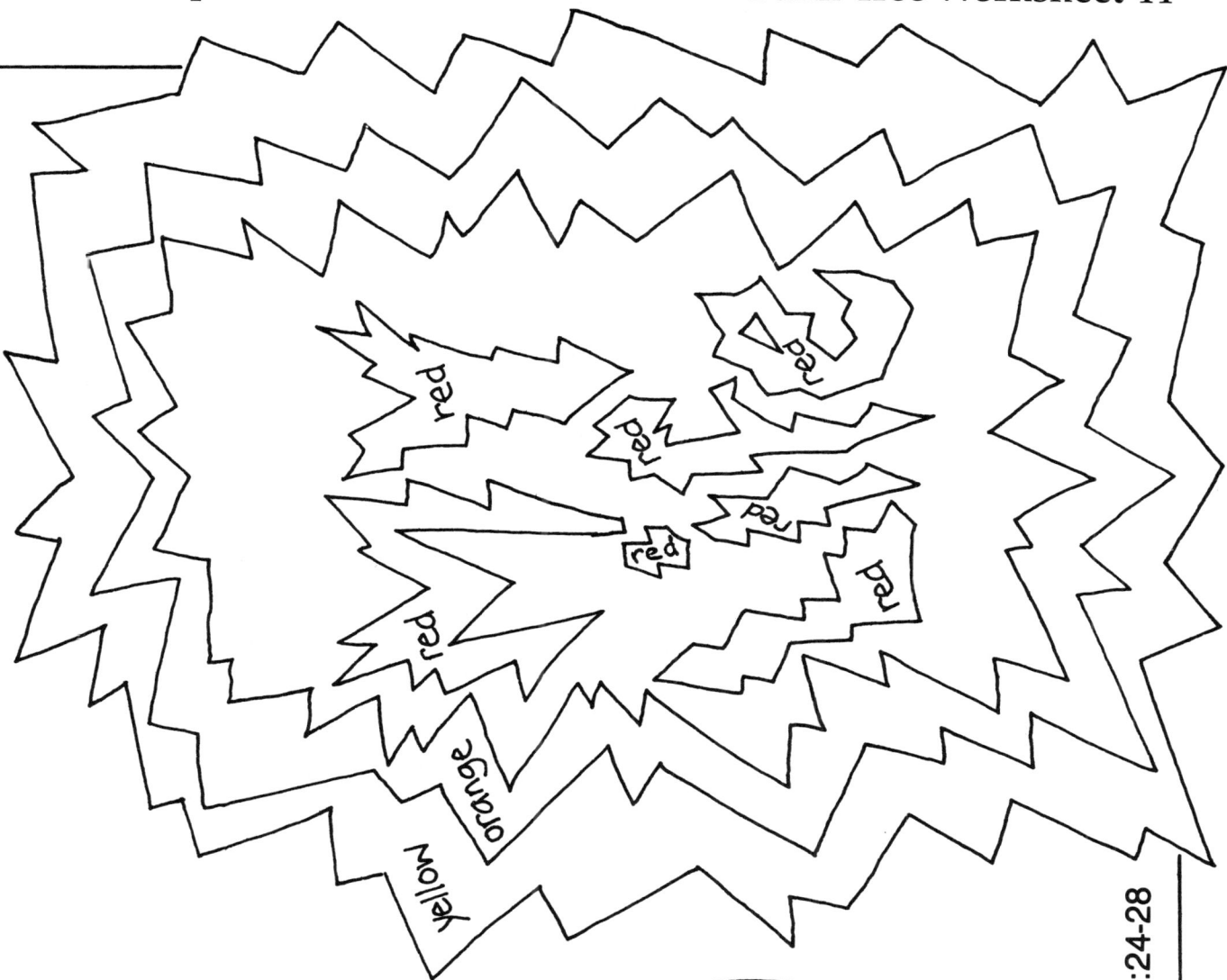

Who is the God we worship?
The one who made the whole universe.
The one who made mountains?

Where is the God we worship?
on a holy mountain?
far away above the sky
very close – we live and move in him

How do we know what God is like?
because we can see him in Jesus
because the world he made shows us his character
because when we pray we start behaving like him

COLOUR THE TRUE SHAPES

Acts 17:24-28

OVERCOME EVIL WITH GOOD.

Romans 12:9-end

Y	R	R	O	S	D	D	A	F	W
A	B	T	S	E	I	R	P	O	D
I	D	F	G	A	E	A	U	R	L
R	S	G	P	C	S	N	P	E	O
A	U	H	I	S	D	H	V	I	H
M	S	G	E	S	O	I	E	G	C
A	A	D	D	L	T	H	N	N	I
S	M	J	O	E	T	R	Q	E	R
M	E	F	O	O	D	E	U	R	E
B	Y	N	G	S	F	T	R	V	J

'A man travelling to JERICHO got MUGGED and left for dead. A PRIEST saw him but PASSED BY. So did a LEVITE. But a FOREIGNER from SAMARIA felt SORRY for the man and washed his WOUNDS and took him to an INN for help. He even PAID for the man's FOOD and SHELTER.' This Samaritan was being a GOOD neighbour. We must DO THE SAME.

Luke 10:25-37

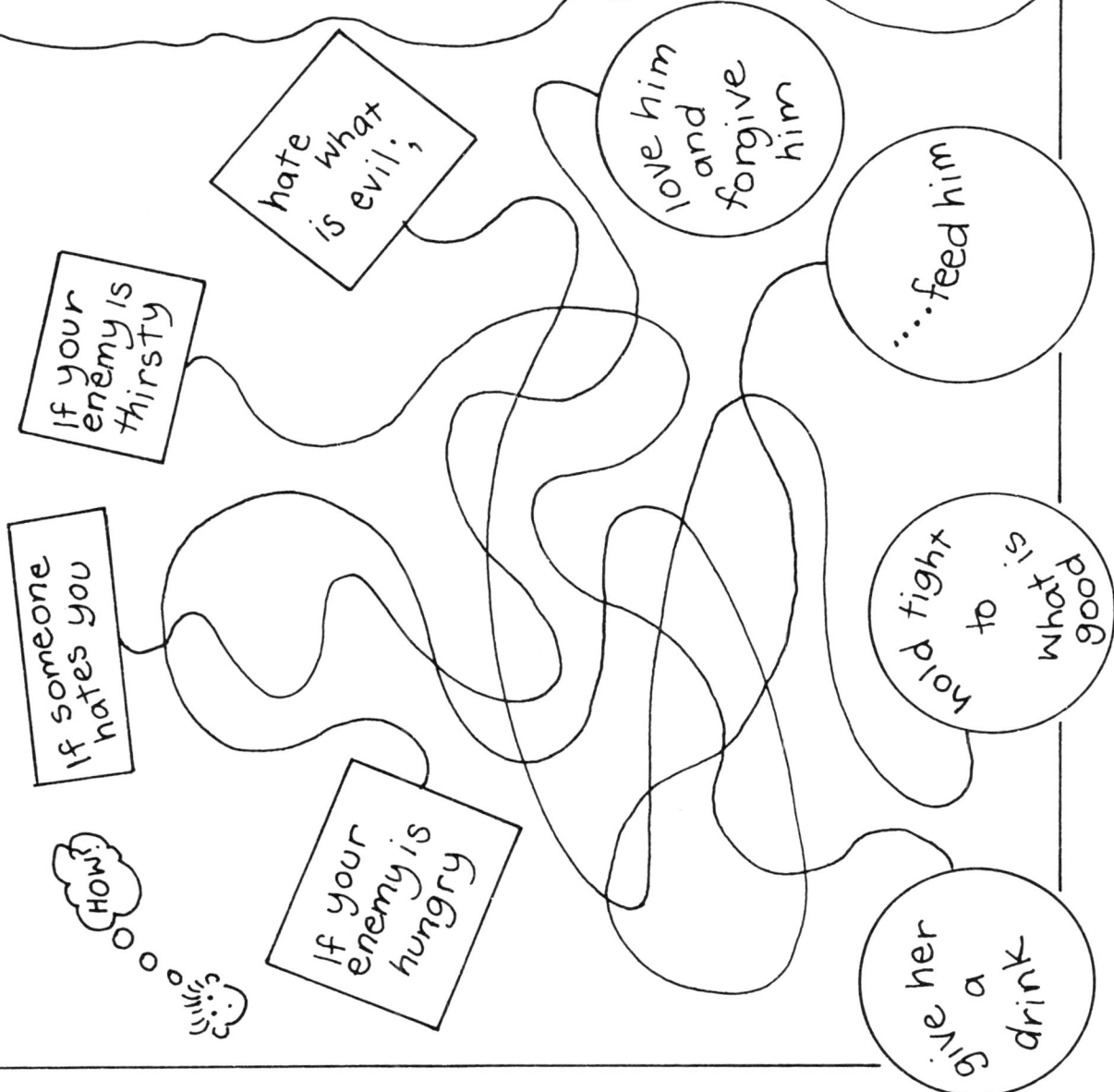

hate what is evil;

If your enemy is thirsty

If someone hates you

If your enemy is hungry

How?

love him and forgive him

...feed him

hold tight to what is good

give her a drink

WE KNOW CHRIST LIVES IN US WHEN WE CARE FOR OTHERS

1 John 3:14

The people of Israel were not allowed to own country. Jeremiah believed they would return home one day. How did he live in their own country. Jeremiah show his faith?

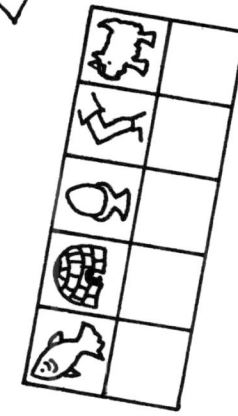

He _____ a _____ in his own country and kept the deeds in an _____ so they would last.

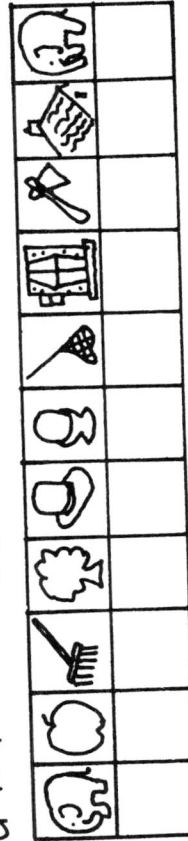

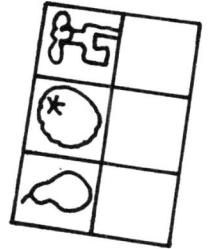

Jeremiah 32:6-15

H	F	C	O	M	M	A	N	D	H
N	A	L	F	L	K	G	S	O	Y
O	L	O	B	N	L	J	M	R	N
I	O	C	O	F	K	E	P	J	W
R	E	W	Q	I	O	S	W	Z	B
U	D	L	O	U	C	U	R	E	D
T	N	A	V	R	E	S	N	M	X
N	O	F	A	I	T	H	T	D	D
E	N	I	A	G	A	H	C	V	A
C	D	E	Z	A	M	A	Y	O	U

Luke 7:1-10

A CENTURION had a SERVANT who was ILL. He sent word to JESUS, 'Sir, I am not WORTHY to have YOU under my ROOF, but just give the COMMAND and I KNOW my servant will be CURED.' Jesus was AMAZED at the man's FAITH. When the messengers got HOME they FOUND the servant completely WELL AGAIN.